This book is a gift—to readers, to the Church, and to the spiritual memoir genre. Preston Yancey writes with stunning clarity, wisdom, and grace, and with this debut sets himself apart as one of the finest writers of faith of our time.
— RACHEL HELD EVANS

I don't know exactly what it is about Preston's writing, but you manage to find a million points of connection no matter how your spiritual path has meandered.... As you turn the very last page, your soul is yearning for God, and you know that he will be found.
— JEN HATMAKER, author of *Interrupted* and
7: An Experimental Mutiny against Excess

Preston's writing is simply gorgeous: clear, elegant, full of emotional honesty. I loved the experiences of curling up with these pages.
— SHAUNA NIEQUIST, author of *Bread & Wine*

As a theologian, Preston is in his own category. He's ancient and modern and skips all the made-up mess in between.... He is brilliant, and this book is a prayer that he has prayed for all of us.
— GLENNON DOYLE MELTON, author of the *New York Times* bestseller
Carry On, Warrior, and the founder of Momastery.com

Many preach grace—Preston practices grace. He loves well and his words engage and dissect the human soul with the precision of a master surgeon.
— JENNIE ALLEN, founder of IF Gathering and author of *Restless*

Preston Yancey is an old soul—I'm allowed to say that because I'm older than he is, but actually I'm humbled and proud to call him a teacher.
— TSH OXENREIDER, author of *Notes From a Blue Bike:
The Art of Living Intentionally in a Chaotic World*

I loved this conflicted, honest, and beautifully written book.
— SARAH BESSEY, author of *Jesus Feminist*

Tables in the Wilderness is a full and rich exploration of the still, quiet, transformative presence of God. Full of wit, wisdom, and emotional gravity, it is a beautiful, spellbinding read from the first word to the last.
— SETH HAINES, editor, deeperstory.com

Journey with Preston Yancey into the bewildering, silent wilderness in this poignant, honest, coming-of-spiritual-age memoir.
— MICHELLE DERUSHA, author of *Spiritual Misfit:
A Memoir of Uneasy Faith*

Preston Yancey deftly explores the intersections of God's voice and his silence, between knowledge and mystery, between brokenness and wholeness. His story is deeply personal, yet shot through with wisdom, theology, liturgy, and quiet.

— ADDIE ZIERMAN, author of *When We Were on Fire: A Memoir of Consuming Faith, Tangled Love, and Starting Over*

Preston's book reads like a carefully crafted novel, replete with unexpected twists that will captive audiences. It is a tale of someone with enough spiritual chops to ask difficult questions about God and life. Read it and uncover a faith worth believing.

— JONATHAN MERRITT, author of *Jesus Is Better Than You Imagined*; senior columnist for Religion News Service

If you know the sound of the silence of God, wrestle to cease striving, and play at spirituality, read *Tables in the Wilderness*. Read it and feel invited in the direction of joy, into the Presence.

— AMBER C. HAINES, blogger at therunamuck and upcoming author with Revell

There are frankly not many contemporary spiritual memoirs anywhere nearly this good (nor this honest).

— JONATHAN MARTIN, author of *Prototype* and founder of Renovatus: A Church for People Under Renovation

It's been a long time since I've read something so beautifully written.

— NISH WEISETH, author of *Speak: How Your Story Can Change the World*, and editor-in-chief, deeperstory.com

Know Preston Yancey for even five minutes, and you'll find yourself longing for a seat next to him around any dinner table.... *Tables in the Wilderness* is a literary morsel to be savored for sure.

— LOGAN WOLFRAM, Executive Director, Allume

Tables in the Wilderness illuminates the simple but essential truth that our place at God's table is that of a welcome and beloved guest, being served a feast not of our design but for our delight.

— KAREN SWALLOW PRIOR, author of *Booked: Literature in the Soul of Me* and *Fierce Convictions: The Extraordinary Life of Hannah More — Poet, Reformer, Abolitionist*

TABLES

IN THE

WILDERNESS

A MEMOIR *of* GOD FOUND,

LOST, *and* FOUND AGAIN

PRESTON YANCEY

ZONDERVAN®

ZONDERVAN

Tables in the Wilderness
Copyright © 2014 by Preston Yancey

This title is also available as a Zondervan ebook.
Visit www.zondervan.com/ebooks.

Requests for information should be addressed to:

Zondervan, 3900 Sparks Dr. SE, Grand Rapids, Michigan 49546

Library of Congress Cataloging-in-Publication Data

Yancey, Preston, 1989-
    Tables in the wilderness : a memoir of God found, lost, and found again /
Preston Yancey.—1st [edition].
        pages   cm
    ISBN 978-0-310-33882-6 (hardcover)
    ISBN 978-0-310-34122-2 (softcover)
    1. Yancey, Preston, 1989- 2. Christian biography—United States. I. Title.
BR1725.Y36A3   2014
277.3'083092—dc23
[B]   2014011391

Cover design: James Hall
Cover photo: Getty Images® / Shutterstock®
Interior design: Katherine Lloyd, The DESK

First Printing August 2014 / Printed in the United States of America

For Hilary
The first time I kiss my wife ...

———⊷⊶———

To Sam, Grant, Antonia, and Jerry

"Best friend isn't a person, Danny.
It's a tier."
— Mindy Kaling

CONTENTS

The answer of course, is that the clock isn't meant to measure earthly time, but the time of the soul. Redemption and condemnation time. For the soul, each instant is always a minute short of judgment.

–Gregory Maguire, *Wicked: The Life and Times of the Wicked Witch of the West*

Gregory of Nyssa points out that Moses's vision of God began with the light, with the visible burning bush, the bush which was bright with fire and was not consumed; but afterwards, God spoke to him in a cloud. After the glory which could be seen with human eyes, he began to see the glory which is beyond and after light. The shadows are deepening all around us.

–Madeleine L'Engle, *A Circle of Quiet*

Because once someone dared
to want you,
I know that we, too, may want you.

–Rilke, *Book of Hours: Love Poems to God*, I, 16

FOREWORD

THE TECHNOLOGICAL REVOLUTION WE have experienced in the last ten years or so has brought about a few unique peculiarities to the publishing world, specifically the Christian one. What I mean is, because of the internet we now have authors, or "content creators," who write books, not just writers. But with this shift there is as ever increasing need for *writers*:

People who have writing in the bones
People whose writing is a part of who they really are
People whose words are beautiful, poetic, deep, and more
than just print on a page

The difference between a content creator and a writer is like the difference between getting a shot of caffeine simply for "fuel" and sipping and savoring on the best cup of Ethiopian Duromina from Stumptown Coffee Roasters for hours. (I'm from Seattle, what can I say.) Preston is a writer. I found myself savoring every word, following this mysterious trail of grace he was laying out on every page. There is something artistic, creative, and beautiful about how his fingers grace the keyboard. I laughed, I wept, and I thought deeply when reading this book.

As someone who's dealt with serious seasons of loneliness, brokenness, and even depression, this book was that very much needed salve of grace. Can God really prepare a table in the wilderness?

Like the Israelites in Psalm 78, I've found myself grumbling, sarcastically or bitterly saying the very same thing. But when reading Preston's words I realized how many times, in our bitter or sarcastic questioning, God's answer is …YES. He really does prepare a table in the wilderness. He prepares a table in the silence. He prepares a table in the depression. He prepares a table in the growing pains. The God of the cosmos prepares a table for you and me.

And we are invited to sit, to eat, to learn, and to laugh.

The funny thing about tables is you sit all the way around them, which means someone is sitting across from you. I always find it interesting that the way our churches are usually set up we are always looking at the back of people's heads. But at a table, we are looking into their eyes. Their face. Their expressions. What a beautiful picture that God not only prepares a table for us, but he sits with us. He looks at us. The God became man and dwelt among us. The Word bowed and tabernacled in our midst.

When you read Preston's words I hope they fill you with as much joy, challenge, and hope as they did for me. For anyone feeling like God is silent, this book is for you. For anyone feeling like they love parts of many denominations but don't know how to sit in that tension, this book is for you.

We are all in the family. We are diverse, we are unique, and we are all the very Body of our King, Jesus. We share the same last name, even though our first names might be different, and that's what matters. The saying goes that "blood is thicker than water" and that saying is true, the only thing is it isn't our blood that unites us but his. And what's best is, like a true family should, we are all invited to the table. The question is, will you have a seat?

Jefferson Bethke

One

SILENCE

WHEN YOU GROW UP evangelical in the South, you hear God speak all the time.

Over the mashed potatoes, under the watch of the calligraphic Scriptures on the walls, in Carl Kasell's voice over the radio on your way to school. You invite God to coffee to study the Bible with you, and God sits beside you on the bus to church camp and laughs at all your jokes. You hear God that night on the jungle gym and that time you stood at the corner downtown with a sandwich in your hand wondering why you got up in the middle of the Ash Wednesday service and fled. And you keep hearing, years on end, even on that Sunday you sit in the parking lot of the small Episcopal church after the Baptist-based ministry you felt God call you to do has crumbled, and you are so vacant and so wavering that you tell God you're done, you're empty, and God tells you to walk into church.

But one September morning, when you least expect it, you're sitting in a friend's apartment after a belated celebration of your twenty-second birthday the night before — in which you read aloud a short story you wrote about lighthouses and champagne, after which your friend tells you you're still in love with the girl you broke up with a year ago and you should call her, find out where things stand—and you're reading the Gospel of Luke when you feel suddenly, keenly, that Christ the Lord is sitting beside you on the couch as you're reading, his voice almost tangible.

"It's going to be about trust with you."

Eight words. Ten syllables.

Then he's gone. And you stop hearing God speak altogether. It's just you, the King James, and the Silence. And you think it might be the middle of something, or the end. Eventually, nearly a year later, you see it as a beginning. But the seeing takes time. For a little while, it's just going to be you and the Silence.

At first, I don't really understand what the silence means.

I was raised Southern Baptist and had stumbled into the Episcopal church on the Feast of Saint Francis my sophomore year at Baylor University and had been living in a two-church—one Baptist, one Episcopalian—Sunday-morning model ever since. Silence in the Baptist church meant you were waiting for God to respond, and in the meantime you were supposed to keep praying and reading the Bible; silence in the Episcopal church meant the same thing; they were just kind enough to write down a few prayers to help see you through.

I try to explain the silence to people outside my friends, to glean perspective, but they tilt their heads and ask if I'm doubting. In their framework, silence is the result of moral failing. It has more to do with me than God. I have stepped away somehow, and they politely hint that it's a secret, unconfessed sin. True, when God is silent you spend some time wondering, and if you're hard-pressed to come up with something, there are plenty of people around you more than willing to shed light on your secret faults. But what I keep trying to explain, and what keeps coming out all tripped and botched, is that I can't call this silence a feeling of absence—which is what they are describing—because as much as I do feel abandoned and alone, I am so stubbornly fixed in the belief that God is omnipresent, ever-loving, and ever-faithful that I can only conclude that God's still hanging around.

God isn't absent, though it feels like God is.

The only word I can form that somehow captures Presence without presence is silence.

It's like the penultimate step before the divorce. You're both in the same room, you're both going about the ordinary routine, but one day you stop talking, stop really seeing each other, and after a little while you just stop trying altogether until one of you gives in and says you want out.

But God doesn't give up, I know that, so I work hard to make sure I don't either.

At first, I go about my normal spiritual business. I read my Bible, I pray, I do all the things you're supposed to do regardless of how you feel. But these things don't appear to be sticking, like they're being cast out upon a pond of ice, bouncing off the frozen top. After a few weeks of ricocheted prayers, I'm lying in bed one morning and I finally address the thought that has been slowly creeping into the back of my mind since the moment on the couch sitting next to Jesus.

While I intellectually know God is still present, while I intellectually know God will never leave me, while I intellectually know God desires the best for me—my heart and my soul, they don't seem so very sure anymore.

God has become an abstract principle; God is there the way calculus is ever truly somewhere; on paper it makes a certain sense, but in the practical, everyday application of going about a life, it doesn't really come up as something I'm inclined to think about and respond to.

And maybe, I wonder quietly aloud, so quietly that I think the words might not even pass beyond breath, *maybe I have stopped believing it altogether.*

Then I wonder why I'm wondering this so quietly.

I started buying prayer books. All kinds of them.

I bought a small, standard, red Book of Common Prayer and started praying the "Daily Devotions for Individuals and Families" because it was short enough to keep my attention span. When Ordinary Time ended and Advent rolled around, some of the daily texts had optional readings from the Apocrypha. I didn't have a Bible with the Apocrypha, so I bought a black leather-bound Book of Common Prayer complete with Bible, Apocrypha, and five fabric bookmarks to help me keep track of it all. Thereafter I took this copy with me to the Episcopal church every Sunday morning and Wednesday evening to prove, vainly, while my faith floundered, that I was that sort of non-Episcopalian Episcopalian who owned his own prayer book. Around then I also started praying "Morning Prayer" and "Evening Prayer," or made an effort to, averaging about two mornings a week and one evening every other month.

I bought a collection of prayers of Saint Francis of Assisi, *The New Oxford Book of Christian Verse*, a collection of daily readings from Madeleine L'Engle, and I rummaged around my stacks and stacks of books until I found one of the eleven copies of *My Utmost for His Highest* people had given me for my high school graduation. I set all of these on the mini-fridge in my dorm room, which doubled as a nightstand. Atop these was a Moleskine journal, a black Pilot Precise V5 pen—thin enough to underline in my Bible without bleeding through the page—and a letter full of poems Samuel, my best friend, had given me one Christmas, which

I used as a kind of icon, a reminder of who I was supposed to be. It doubled as a bookmark.

I invented an elaborate routine in which I read the selections from L'Engle, Chambers, and then the daily lectionary and spent several moments of contemplative thought shooting up theological rumination toward the heavens, hoping God would decide to put a check mark next to one of them, something to let me know God was still around and not simply in the abstract way.

But for all my prayer books, my devotionals, my Samuel-icon letters and V5-precise pens, nothing seemed to be happening.

I found that I spent a lot of time thinking *about* God and talking *about* God, but slowly any formal or informal dialogue *with* God felt more pointless than it ever had before. Every time I began, I felt caught against the veil that had settled between us, the veil of God's silence, and I didn't know how to break through.

I bought more books. I bought a shameful amount of books. I bought books about the theology of eating as it related to Communion, art history studies of images of the Virgin Mary in the late Middle Ages, Karl Barth's complete *Church Dogmatics*, and more books by Anne Lamott and Madeleine L'Engle than I could count. After a while, I stopped reading the books I was buying. They formed teetering piles in my room, lined my shelves, and filled a massive copper basin from the 1930s my paternal grandmother had given me when she was moving out of her house.

"What will you use it for?" she asked.

"I can put books in it," I stated matter-of-factly, as if it was the most obvious use for an antique copper basin.

My books and I lived in the silence of God for a time. Every once in a while I would pick one up, read a few pages, and lay it aside when the feeling of Presence did not return. I'm not sure what I expected to happen, if I imagined that I would come across a cluster of words like an incantation and the Holy Spirit would rouse like a corpse within me, but I did, in some way, think that if I surrounded myself with all this proof that people had felt God, were still feeling God, then I could, someday, feel God again too.

Crina and I meet for coffee midwinter in the rain when she gets back from spending the fall semester in Europe. We catch up on the usual complaints—she's studying for the MCAT, I'm trudging through thesis research; she doesn't have any time to read Dante, I'm afraid I might die alone.

Eventually our conversation circles around to talking about God. Crina shares about her time away, surrounded by a group of girls who all seem keenly aware of God's Presence.

"But I don't feel God like that," Crina says.

"Neither do I, right now," I confess.

"What's wrong with us?"

I pause a second and stare into my nearly drained cappuccino cup, watching a few bubbles of foam burst. "Maybe this is just a season." I say this hoping, but I don't sound hopeful. "Maybe it's forever." I say this honestly, because I'm starting to think it. "I'm not entirely sure. What I know is that right now, I don't doubt that God exists; I don't doubt that God is good; what I doubt is myself. I doubt that I can even hear God, maybe I doubt that I have ever heard God." Because even when I think about Jesus on that couch a handful of months ago, even when I think about those words about trust, it's a fuzzy kind of figment blur, as easily explained away as it is believed in.

"I hate the silence," Crina murmurs.

"I do too."

And we sit there, in our respective silences, for ten minutes or so before we abandon our coffee and agree to see each other again in a few weeks, after the holidays, using the good, oft-ironic idiom, "When things have calmed down."

⋈

A parenthetical.

I need to explain something about written prayers.

Not everyone needs the Book of Common Prayer; not everyone needs their prayers to have been written down. But I do. I, with all my many stacks of books about God and love and presence, I need the written prayers. Not because I feel unqualified to pray, but because for a little while I don't think that I could. When I went to pray, I stumbled around all my own wants and my own cares and talked more to myself than to God.

The written prayers reminded me, still remind me—force me at times—to pray obediently for the neighbors I would have forgotten, perhaps purposefully, to name. They make me pray for the whole world. They make me pray for my own vagabond heart to hear God through the Scripture truly and rightly.

I need written prayers because otherwise I become too comfortable with my own haphazard version of grace. Because I need the wisdom of the thousands gone before me who forgot to pray for their neighbors too, who were wise enough to write down the reminder that it needs doing, that those prayers need praying just as much as the prayers for food to be nourishment to our bodies and for the stoplight to stay green as we speed through.

When I first felt God stop speaking, I spent a lot of time looking for quotes that would inspire me back to hearing. In mid-Advent I was rereading the letters of Simone Weil and I stopped over her words, "The action of grace in our hearts is secret and silent."[1]

Grace, this formative power conforming me into the image of a God I could no longer feel, was something come from the silence. But the silence of God can feel like a kind of wilderness, and you're staggering around begging *Water!* where there is none to be had.

Another psalm speaks of the Israelites wandering in the desert before they entered the Promised Land, "Then they spoke against God; They said, 'Can God prepare a table in the wilderness?' "[2]

Eventually, I stop trying. For the most part. I give up on the whole idea of prayer, except for Sundays and Wednesdays during the Episcopal liturgy and in the appointed times for free prayer with the Baptists, because outside of those times I don't feel inclined if God is just going to keep silent the entire time. But I keep going to church. I keep forcing myself to read along with the liturgy. The reasons for it slip and slide. One week it's about appearance, and the next it has to do with a belief that the words are sticking, are making something happen within me that otherwise could not come to pass, that the Holy Spirit really does pray on our behalf with groans we don't understand.

It's not much, but I at least commit twice a week to keeping myself marginally connected to the Center.

In *Walking on Water*, Madeleine L'Engle tells a parable about a town that lets all their clocks run and run without ever winding them. Eventually, all the clocks break. When the Watchmaker comes, he refuses to repair their clocks because the townspeople never looked after the clocks in the first place.

I don't feel I can do much, but I can keep my clock wound. I can go to church every Sunday and Wednesday, I can cross myself, I can lift my hands, I can bow toward the altar, I can receive Communion.

I can at least keep the clock wound.

If only my life were structured so that I had to deal with God and God's quiet just twice a week. What I study in school, what I blog about, what I spend nearly every ordinary conversation some-how addressing all has to do with, specifically, relating the whole of a person and our lives to God. God is unavoidable, but God feels completely removed.

One Sunday morning in the liturgy we pray,

Open, O Lord, the eyes of all people to behold thy gra-cious hand in all thy works, that, rejoicing in thy whole creation, they may honor thee with their substance, and be faithful stewards of thy bounty.

And I find that I'm weeping, because it's a prayer for those who have yet to know God at all, but I've stumbled into praying it for myself.

Sometime later, much later, I read in the Psalms one morning that the Lord speaks: "Be still, and know that I am God; I will be exalted among the nations; I will be exalted in the earth."[3]

I wonder what sort of stillness you must have to truly hear.

There's a moment in Exodus in which we read that the Lord commanded the people to consecrate themselves to prepare to receive God at Mount Sinai. After two days of cleansing, "Moses brought the people out of the camp to meet God."[4]

The Israelites stood at the base of the mountain as lightning flashed and thunder roared, a thick cloud veiling its peak. Then the Lord descended in fire, and smoke billowed up into the heavens while the whole of the mountain shook. Moses speaks to God, and God answers him from the thunder and calls Moses to meet God at the top of the mountain, so Moses goes. God tells Moses to let the people come only so close, for God is holy and God's glory wondrous, such that it might kill them to behold it. When Moses returns, he tells the people all God has said, and then something remarkable happens, the beauty of which never occurs again in the whole of the Scripture.

"Then God spoke all these words, saying, 'I am the Lord your God, who brought you out of Egypt.'"[5] And then God gives the commandments to the people.

Never again does God gather people around a mountain and so awesomely, so clearly, communicate. Here, God reveals the Ten Commandments, speaks the laws that govern creation before the chosen people, the people created, and it is as if God has once again called forth light into being when before light was not.

Later, I would hear Lauren Winner talk about this moment in Scripture. She explained that the first letter of the commandments God speaks to the people is the Hebrew letter *aleph*, which is not a letter that produces a sound, but a glottal stop. It is a letter of silence. When God speaks the commandments to the Israelites from the mountain, in the midst of all that fire and lightning, the first sound God gives them is the sound of God's silence.[6]

Then after the silence comes the declaration and the promise, "'I am the Lord your God.'"

In the midrash on this portion of Exodus, it says, "Rabbi Abbahu said in the name of Rabbi Yohanan: When God gave the Torah no bird twittered, no fowl flew, no ox lowed, none of the Ophanim stirred a wing, the Seraphim did not say, 'Holy, Holy,' the sea did not roar, the creatures spoke not, the whole world was hushed into breathless silence and the Voice went forth: I am the Lord your God."[7]

What is the silence of God? It is preparatory and expectant. Israel knows God has brought them to the base of the mountain to make Godself known to them. In the space of time, but a moment in reality, in which God makes no sound, it might very well seem that eons pass in silence, but out from it comes the Word of God.

Afterward, Moses tells the people, "God has come in order to test you."[8] The test is in this moment of silence. It is in the moment in which God is present and yet seemingly withheld, near enough to behold but veiled behind a curtain of quiet. In this space, as the earth keeps silent vigil, God tests the people to see if they should believe, even in silence, that God has come to dwell with them.

In turn, the people keep silent, for God, in quiet or speech, is before them.

"Be still, and know that I am God."

I suppose that if you're a good, spiritual person, the kind of person who fears that accidentally killing a butterfly could somehow wound the cosmos, you fill the Silence by staying rooted in the Scripture, praying consistently, and trusting that God is still speaking even when you can't seem to hear. At least, this is what reading the saints has led me to believe.

If you're like me, having similar feelings about the butterfly for about three hours a week and the rest of the time you are otherwise actively ambivalent, you read Scripture only when you can't bear not to, because your best friend is going to ask if you've been keeping up and you can't lie to him. And you've already stopped praying, because it feels like the most pointless and unproductive use of your time. You look around and see all the shiny, happy people who seem to be hearing God through every little brush of wind and flap of butterfly wings and wonder if everyone is crazy and you're the only one who is sane or—worse—you're the only crazy one and everyone else is sane.

So you compensate. You overcompensate.

You talk about God all the time. To everyone. To everything. You talk about God in the coffee shop, over burgers, in line at the grocery store, to the receptionist at the doctor's office when your insomnia has reached the point that it's time to seek professional help. You do anything and everything that keeps you talking *about* God instead of *to* God. If you can fill the Silence with your words, if you can keep chattering away long enough, maybe you won't have to deal with what comes out of the Silence, the loneliness that sinks in so deep you think it will smother your soul, the wondering if you'll ever feel something beyond this Silence again.

You make do, for a little while, with your incessant chatter, your stacks of books, and your twice a week forced liturgical prayer.

"What first brought you to attend St. Paul's?" Someone asks me this at a party, where we drink wine out of plastic cups and make small talk about our favorite beach reading, which I unfortunately ruin by mentioning a book about feminine spirituality in the High Middle Ages. I've told the story of coming to St. Paul's Episcopal Church enough times to enough complete strangers that the answer comes as rote: "I told God that I was empty and that I needed a place to hide, to be filled."

"And now?" He squeezes his plastic cup slightly and the wine, like the wine in Communion, lifts up to the rim.

I hesitate. I know the answer I'm supposed to give, something about being filled and renewed and able to journey forward without sinking into despair. I have given this answer before, many times, but today I can't form the words. As I stare at the wine in the plastic cup, as I can't help but think of it as Communion wine, as the wine that is somehow Other, is called the Blood of Christ, shed for us, shed for me, to keep me in everlasting life, I realize that I'm not on a journey, I'm still hiding.

"I guess I'm waiting to see."

I say it more to the wine than to the person asking me.

⋈

Before, sometime in October, when I was starting to buy all those prayer books, on our way to lunch, I tell Dr. Wood about the ideas I have for a book. Dr. Wood has seen me through a lot over the years, perhaps most notable being that he is the reason I began to read saints. In his Christian Spirituality course, I sat on the front row and painstakingly tried to get through every reading, filling notebook after notebook with all kinds of loose but lucid ideas. Thoughts on the atonement, on art, on the fullness of the body and soul in harmony. When he called on me, I would tentatively answer, dumbly, things like, "Arianism?" and he would jovially thunder in response, "Exactly! Substitutionary atonement!" because he is both deaf as a post and as passionate as wildfire.

I tell him that in the book I hoped to write, I want to begin by talking about silence, the silence of God and the silence of ourselves, about how we must learn a particular kind of silence in order to be read by Scripture instead of simply reading it for our own devices.

" 'Be still and know that I am God,' " I quote, making the point.

"You know what that really means in the Hebrew?" Dr. Wood asks. "It means, *Shut up!*"

I didn't understand it then, or perhaps I didn't want to understand it, so I made a noise of agreement and then kept rambling on about all the things I knew about God.

Remember your baptism.

That was another thing I learned from Dr. Wood. He liked to tell us that when someone had fallen into sin or fallen into the silence of God, what they should be told to do is to remember their baptism. Baptism, because the moment of conversion can be tricky. Remembering which of the hundred thousand times I prayed to ask Jesus into my heart, which is the evangelical way of phrasing it, is difficult. I can't tell you which one of those counted as the exact moment the Holy Spirit came in and took up residence. But I can tell you about my baptism. Dr. Wood pointed out that remembering our baptism is remembering that there was a moment in which we affirmed, without question, that the good work of the Holy Spirit had begun in our lives. It would see us through. If you are in sin, remember your baptism, in which you professed that you would renounce evil and cling ever and always to the mercy and goodness of Christ. If you are in the shadow of God, if God is silent, if God seems to be absent, remember your baptism, in which it was confirmed that you were indeed of God's own and held safely.

In the silence, I start thinking about my own baptism.

Our Baptist church was meeting at the YMCA because we sold our old building—I think to Methodists, but I'm likely fabricating that—and were building a new one. I was five and in the swimming pool with my father, the pastor.

There were tears in his eyes as he held me. "Into his death," he said in the words of Saint Paul as he dipped me into the water. Chlorine stung my eyes and a bubble escaped my nose. I was only under a moment, as death surely is itself, but the silence of it was incredible. There is silence when we are buried with Christ.

When I broke up from the water, all splash and grace, the assembled congregation clapped, filled the space with loud, vibrant joy, and chased the silence away.

Remember your baptism.

It's Christmas Eve, and I have left our full and lively dinner table to drive ten miles out of town to an Episcopal church to attend Christmas Vigil. It's already been a full night, juggling carpools as we caravanned to the candlelight service at the Baptist church my parents are members of before we crowded around the table at home to eat the family tradition of prime rib. It's a storm-laden night, and around eleven, I brave the rain and make the drive to church.

Christmas is one of my favorite times of year, that time when we mark the beauty and mystery of the God who suddenly, impossibly, broke into our midst in the Incarnation. But I feel nothing.

The Episcopal church is named Trinity because of the massive stained glass of Rublev's Trinity that overlooks the altar in the nave. Father, Son, and Spirit sit together around a table, distinguished only by the color of their robes, iconographically suspended in an eternal conversation and exchange. Three but One. Full, abundant, and ever connected to the Whole. In another season, I should see the beauty in this. But this Christmas Eve, this time in which we mark the marvel of all marvels, when I look into the Trinity what I see is not the three faces of the One God. What I see is the darkened, obscured, silent faces that are concealed in the quiet hour before Light comes into the world.

We hold candles in our hands, pass light from one to another, fill the space with tiny flames that testify to the great and coming Mystery that is breaking into our midst. I feel dead and weary and alone. Each motion staged, every word forced. I cross myself against myself, I cross myself as a kind of halfhearted prayer, willing body to enact what soul cannot seem to muster.

> *Let all mortal flesh keep silence,*
> *   And with fear and trembling stand;*
> *Ponder nothing earthly minded,*
> *   For with blessing in His hand,*
> *Christ our God to earth descendeth,*
> *   Our full homage to demand.*

We sing this before the midnight hour, before we say that Christ has come and our little candle lights join the whole of the nave, bathed in light, and the *Alleluias* and *Joy to the Worlds* begin.

The canticle is taken from the prophet Habakkuk, "But the Lord is in His holy temple. Let all the earth be silent before Him."[9]

Habakkuk, the same prophet who calls out to God, "How long, O Lord, will I call for help, And You will not hear?"[10]

We sing about God's presence among us in the coming of Christ. We sing and we sing, and I keep hoping, somehow, that the remembrance of God's coming will bring God back to me. I hold my candle, I sing Alleluia, but God does not reach beyond the veil. God does not move close enough to whisper.

When I leave the service, I turn my phone on and pick through a few emails and tweets in the parking lot before I come across a text from Samuel, two hours behind me spending Christmas with his family in Seattle, and the phrase that lingers in the midst of his message about heading into Christmas Vigil probably the same time as I was walking out of it, "I'll keep watch for us."

I drive in silence the way home, miss my exit, and have to double back a few miles. I turn over that phrase in my mind again and again, Samuel's promise that he'd keep the vigil for us both, because he knew that in the moment I couldn't. And I realize all the people along the way who have been keeping the vigil for me when I could not: parents who pray for things they don't know to pray for; Antonia, Jerry, and Grant, friends so deep it can hurt to breathe against that kind of love, who pray when they see me sitting in the coffee shop reading through my stacks of books, hoping that somewhere in them I glimpse God again. And I start to think, too, ridiculously, that those stacks of books, those stacks of icon books, are in a sense praying for me too. That I have been surrounded, all over, by people and things that were fashioned by the hands of the Creator and that, because of this and this alone, they somehow are keeping the vigil for me too.

><

Time moves strangely in the Gospels. In the Gospel of Luke, Jesus is born and then a sentence later is being presented at the Temple, but in reality forty days separate the events. Because they're so close, I find myself spending Christmastide thinking about the earliest moments in the life of Jesus. I meander through the stories and dwell in strange places. I pray, halfheartedly, in the way I can still pray, crooked arrow shots toward the vaulted heavens, that God would give me imagination again, the sort of imagination that would help me love Scripture once more, to glimpse God, even in silence, within the words. A few days before Epiphany I read over the presentation of Christ and stop when I come to the story of Simeon and Anna. Simeon had been promised by God that he would not die before he saw the Messiah. He sees Christ in the arms of Mary, praises the coming redemption of Israel, warns Mary of the wound that shall come to her own heart for what Jesus must suffer, and then glorifies God, saying that he may depart the world in peace, having seen the promised redemption.

But Anna is a different story altogether. What we are told of Anna is that she was a faithful woman, had been married seven years and then widowed, and lived to the age of eighty-four. She spent all her time as a widow in the Temple, fasting and praying. After Simeon's exclamation comes Anna's, seeing the Christ child and somehow knowing that he has come. She praises God and tells everyone around her of the wonders that God has done.

We don't know whether Anna had the same promise as Simeon; we don't know if God had told her she would glimpse the glory unfolding. About Anna, all we really know is that she was faithful and that after eighty-four years of a faithful life, she unexpectedly encountered Christ.

I wonder about Anna. I wonder about those eighty-four years. I wonder if they were silent years. I wonder if they were years of the quietest kind of faithfulness. And I wonder if I can do it. I wonder if I can keep being faithful, even if it's just forced prayer twice a week, stacks of icon books, and all these people keeping vigil for me. I wonder if maybe after my eighty-four years, someday, again, I'll glimpse Christ.

I'm getting coffee with Eileen, who is the kind of research librarian you think you'll only ever see in movies. One semester I was working on iconography of the Virgin Mary in Anglo-Norman France between the ninth and thirteenth centuries and had seen an image in an otherwise out-of-date and poorly sourced book that would have been perfect for my argument. It was Eileen who called museums, emailed a nunnery in France, and tracked down the diptych leaf of Mary and Child that had otherwise been thought to be lost. It had been stored in a reliquary, with those French nuns, who gave me permission to use it and provided the bibliographic reference.

"I think God is like a kaleidoscope," she says, sipping her tea because she doesn't have a taste for coffee. "God is unchanging, but we're standing on the image we see. One day we wake up and find that God has shifted the image. Everything looks different. The world looks different. The world seems new. The trick is learning how to recognize that all the old colors are still there. It's just the patterns that have changed."

During Epiphany I meet with my spiritual director, Barbara. We have been meeting for about a year. When I was first introduced to her in the small room adjoining the nave, she had drawn three chairs into a small triangle. Taking one and indicating that I should take one as well, she waited for me to be seated and then gestured to the third chair.

"This," she explained, "is for the Holy Spirit."

Her point was clear. God is always present. Present in every place and at every time, more sensed in some places than others. The third chair was the reminder of that continual, perpetual, ever Presence.

The Presence that right now I cannot feel.

The chair is an icon, a reminder that when Barbara and I speak to one another, this can be prayer.

Barbara is a tiny woman, graciously wrinkled, with kind eyes. When we meet each month, she lights a candle, lays a cross beside it, and waits in silence in her chair as I take my own. When we are finished and I am ready to leave, she prays for me. She thanks God for me. She prays more for what is to come than what we have talked about. According to Barbara, the third chair has meant that we have been praying about the things we talked about for that hour. So at the close, we have no need to pray again on those things. They have been prayed for.

When I've left in the past, I have gone unburdened, even when I didn't come feeling oppressed. I have encountered for a moment how *chronos*, human time, time which is linear to us and we move forward in progressively, intersects with *kairos*, divine time, time which does not move forward in seconds and minutes but in vertical directions and in circles. For it is in this place where the real that we know, the real of tables and desks and chairs and lattes and Netflix and subways, and the Real that we are meant to know, the Real of Angels and Beauty and Glory and Light and Truth and Grace, converge, or come so close to touching that you can tell, in an instant of *chronos* time and in an eternity of *kairos* time, that the Presence is more felt in that space than in others.

But I can no longer feel God. I tell Barbara about this, again, after months of telling her. I tell her about forcing myself to pray. I tell her about my icon stack of prayer books and theology. I tell her about the people I think are keeping vigil for me. I tell her about everything I have tried to do to bring Jesus back, to convince him to unpack the boxes and live in this space with me again, instead of just hanging around, but that he's not coming back, that he's standing around and refusing to speak. I told her about Jesus on the couch, about the trust, about how I managed a few months on handicapped prayers before I slipped completely into wordless ambivalence.

Barbara studies me.

"As has just been said: 'Today, if you hear his voice, do not harden your hearts as you did in the rebellion.'"[11]

She says it quietly, calmly, but her eyes pierce me.

"What else have I been doing?" I nearly shout. She has quoted the anonymous epistle to the Hebrews. She's pointed to the passage about the Israelites grumbling against God as God led them through the desert.

"God's not talking. What is there to hear?"

Barbara considers me, seems to see something that wasn't there before.

"Can God prepare a table in the wilderness?"

A few months ago, I had shared that scrap from Psalm 78 and said something about maybe it keeping me afloat, back before I started buying the prayer books and filling my time with talking *about* God instead of *to* God.

"Yes," I respond sheepishly but annoyed. I mean *yes* intellectually. *Yes* as in it's the thing you're supposed to say.

"Can God prepare a table in the wilderness?" she asks again, refusing to break my gaze.

"Yes." Now I'm frustrated. I'm staring at the third chair, the empty third chair.

"Can God," she asks a third time, "prepare a table in the wilderness?"

"Of course! Of course God can! God does all the time for

everyone else, but right now God has not chosen to prepare one for me."

There are tears, tears that I had not expected.

Barbara raises her hand, and, with the movement, my tears stop.

"This is the table," she speaks simply, taking her free hand and casting it over the empty space between us, in the midst of the three chairs.

"This is the table, Preston. It's time for you to stop spending all your time trying to get God back and realize that God truly is right here, right in your midst, and God's spread a table before you. Maybe this is how God is speaking to you. In the icon stack. In the faces of those keeping vigil for you. Maybe, maybe it's time for you to stop chattering away and finally keep silent so that you can actually *hear* God whisper. Stop doing. Stop striving. Stop."

She holds up both hands, commanding.

"You're in the middle space. You're on the plateau. Here is the table before you. This is the wilderness. You have arrived somewhere. God has brought you to somewhere. He said it would be about trust, and, you see, it is. You're in this somewhere space, this wilderness space." She sits back in her chair and gives me a solemn nod. "Now, go have a look around."

Two

BEGINNINGS

ALL OF THAT HAPPENED my senior year at Baylor.
But I need to go back a bit before I can go forward.
Some things need explaining.

I am not sure when I became a Christian.

What I am sure of is that the language of the gospel was woven throughout my home long before I was born, and long after too. I am sure that I was raised to know Jesus as well as my own name. I am sure that the songs, the stories, the art, the laughter, was all held so loosely and yet so firmly in the palm of grace.

When I was born in Dallas, Texas, my father was a pastor of a medium-sized Southern Baptist church, and my mother served as a consultant for Fortune 500 companies, teaching office oversight, best practices, and stress management. After my mother went back to work, my father would bring me up to the church with him instead of putting me into day care. Looking back on this, I do not see two people who overly invested in their child or made me feel like I was always being watched, but who believed in the old and deep magic of presence and proximity, who believed in the unspoken parts of faith, communicated in and by nearness, prayer as action as much as word.

My mother says that there was a time when I was about three that she was pushing me around in a shopping cart in the store where you used to be able to buy ICEEs and warm pretzels, when I looked at her seriously and said I wanted to ask Jesus into my heart.

She was, rightfully, a bit skeptical. She and my father spent a long time praying about and discussing it, and over the next handful of years frequently asked me what I thought that meant, what I understood of this Jesus, trying to discern what I could connect to at such a young age.

I remember, in the interim, being awake in the late evening in the dark of my room, the yellow glow of the sodium street lamp on the corner fractured by the blinds, and winding the same prayer over and over, the short one that was supposed to untangle all things eternal. I did not think it hadn't taken the first or hundredth time, but I didn't think there was any hurt in repeating it.

Dear Jesus, come into my heart and be my Lord and Savior. Amen.

(In hindsight, it's not a bad prayer to pray more than once.)

The watershed for my parents was when, a few years later, I was with one of my aunts, volunteering with her church at a retirement home — *volunteering* may be an extremely generous term to describe my actions at five. In front of a group of retired seniors, I took a microphone and informed them of how they could have a personal relationship with Jesus Christ, that he could come live in their hearts, and that they would go to heaven.

My aunt called my parents that afternoon to tell them, adding that if there was any indication I had converted and whatever the ramifications of that were for someone so young, it was surely confirmed in this moment.

So when did it happen? When was I once something and then forever something else?

I cannot think of the moment, the exact moment, when the Holy Ghost descended and dwelt, whether it was in that shopping cart or during one of those conversations or on that little makeshift stage with that microphone, but sometime during that or before that or just on the heels of it, conversion happened. Or at least the first steps of conversion happened.

I have already written about my baptism, but it has me remembering the church that met at the YMCA.

They are a people who pray.

A people who lift hands during the upbeat songs and lift them higher during the mournful. They sing all the best hymns and all the best new songs, and the lyrics of those songs season the way I pray. If the Baptists do not have a prayer book, they have a hymnal, and that hymnal is its own sort of liturgy, its own sort of vocabulary of prayer and habit of being.

> I will run to the cleft of the mountain and wait for You
>   there.
> Will You come and meet with me?[12]

The line circles back and haunts me in the silence. It's an easy thing to sing when it is abstract, a plea for God to pass by when you have certainty that God will. But when you are uncertain, and you are uncertain that you should even want to run to that cleft, the exercise seems a lie.

In the secret, in the quiet place.
In the stillness You are there.[13]

In the stillness You are there.

When you sing *in the stillness*, I think you forget what stillness is.

There is a Sunday, or perhaps a conflation of many Sundays, when I am standing in the tiled room with the padded chairs, Abigail up at the electric keyboard with her wrinkled hands, spinning out the lyric prayers. My father, his deep voice near the front about to preach, joy spilling off him. I am standing by my mother, because I can hear her in memory, in that delicate way she sings, and I press the recollection. I can feel again what it is that I believe I feel then, a first encounter, or perhaps earliest remembered encounter, with the Presence of God.

But thou art holy, O thou that inhabitest the praises of Israel.[14]

In this room with the lifted hands, on this Sunday or these many Sundays, with Abigail's hands spinning the electric keys into prayer, there the Presence of God dwells. Not only in the words but also in the floor and the walls and the covered chairs and the lifted hands. It is as if the world has a different texture, that to see the ordinary is nonetheless to see God, and it is a sort of mystical experience without mystical consequence: this is simply church. It is quiet in a way, even with the lifted hands and songs of praise; it is expectation that should the people of God gather, God is Present. Perhaps not felt, but God *is*.

What this church gives me, among so many other things, is the reassurance of meaning. Something is instilled in me that should all else be for naught, should all of these things of faith, these things we profess to believe, somehow not be true, the world spinning out toward the dark and the abandoned, then there is still a purpose in lifting hands and singing the old songs. Because in this God is there. That is enough.

For I shall yet praise him.[15]

Notice.

A sparse, glimpsed narrative. I am recording and recounting the more obvious moments of God's breaking into the midst of my ordinary. There were plenty of ordinary times between those moments, ordinary times of baking and reading, of spilling sauce down my shirt or burning my wrist on an iron that was left on that looks, to this day, like I tried to take a blade to myself.

Notice that what I have given you is an account of the ordinary that was known to me at the time, that it was not unexpected for God to slip into my midst, to announce, to annunciate. I'm telling you to notice, because at a certain point I stopped. At a certain point I stopped noticing that God was moving all around me, and I believe it was this lack of attention on my part, this willingness to treat common the awe of the Almighty, that would eventually arrive me to a place where God withdrew.

Notice: the lifted hands, the still, small voice, the shaky prayers. All of this was a sort of ordinary. Until it wasn't.

Sometime when I was in the middle of first grade, our family moved from Dallas to San Antonio so my father could become the pastor of a church on the northeast side of the city. Shortly after our move, my mother was unpacking boxes in our new home when she lifted a heavy trunk poorly, which caused a handful of nerves in her back to pinch and white hot pain to pulsate over

TABLES in the WILDERNESS

her body. From that point on, in the years that followed, a series of unfortunate events with physical therapists, well-meaning but misguided doctors, allergic reactions to pharmaceuticals, trips to Mayo Clinic that resulted in more questions than answers, resulted in my mother being diagnosed with Complex Regional Pain Syndrome (CRPS), a very misunderstood condition in which a person develops a persistent, chronic burning pain in one of their limbs.

(This is the definition on the Mayo Clinic website, as well as the National Health Institute website. I have memorized it.)

Except my mother didn't develop CRPS in one of her limbs. Those haphazard visits and sessions and medical treatments resulted in the disease spreading to her entire body, leaving her with the feeling that she was chronically being set aflame all over, from the top of her head to the soles of her feet.

The timing of things.

The woman who used to demand that we spend most Saturdays in museums and galleries was now increasingly bedridden. The woman who taught professionalism and management strategies for large corporations was no longer able to drive. I learned that we come to expect the comfort we never believe we'll lose. We vacationed less. Dad had to work more to make up for the income hit. Life as we knew it slowly unraveled and evolved into a shape that didn't resemble what it was before.

We made it work, we found our way, but it was slow going.

Over the course of the next several years there were moments in which God broke in and through. Promises and confirmation of promises that my mother would be miraculously healed this side of eternity—be it by the miracle of science or the miracle of a moment. Thirteen Scriptural promises were slowly given, things to stand on, concrete claims of God's generous and wild love.

This is hard to explain. This is hard to return to.

I could tell you of the times that were hard. The tears. The moments when the pain seemed to swallow the mortal tent with a vengeance. I could tell you about the time the deacon who hated my father accused him of a "secret sin" that was causing my mother to be bedridden, how my parents thought I didn't know it had happened at the time, how I nearly stomped on the man's foot the next time I saw him. I could tell you what it means when you're an only child in a house where one parent seems abandoned by God on an island bed and how you start reading every book you can lay hold of because another world would surely be better than this one. How you learn to do laundry, to cook, to reach for the things that are too high or to bend for the things that fell down, to fear and dread speed bumps when driving. How when you use the handicap decal when parking and get out of the car with young, formed legs, people stare until you open the passenger door and the woman who is still so young sets a cane firmly down upon the pavement before rising.

Those are the facts, but the relevant truth, the piece of this you need to know, is what my parents showed me in the midst of this.

My father's best friend was bedridden, but he loved her fiercely and wildly and beautifully and kept her laughing and let her be angry and let her cling. He showed me what it meant to love into the darkness of grief, and he carried my own emotional wounds, a child uncertain of what was to come, and he whispered the mercy of God against my head night after night and told me the old stories were the truest stories, that God held all things.

And my mother? My mother spent her days as she spends them now, writing letters to every person she has ever met, offering them love and encouragement and peace. She's hours on the phone praying for others, doing the slow work of offering thanksgiving or championing the Light or interceding with that "hedge of protection," a phrase that haunts my prayers with a beauty that seems unfair to try and lay hold of.

But it does something to you, to have a chronically ill parent, a parent who does not die but clings on to life in spite of pain that pierces to bone. It does something to faith, rips it away or buries it deep.

I'm worried about this portion of the narrative.

I am worried about whether or not it is honest. What I am handing over is at best highlights, big moments, thumping things that ring loud. I am trying to condense about eighteen years of self into a handful of words, and I worry that it will come off as nothing more than bullet points of big moments before settling back into the steady rhythm of unfolding self.

This has me thinking about Scripture.

Scripture trips over ordinary, over uneventful, and gives it a passing glance. We are told that so-and-so gave birth and a verse later the child is grown. But how eventful is pregnancy, is the carrying to term, the moment of birth, the first trembling and uncertain steps and all before, after, and between? Scripture isn't concerned with conveying the ordinary. It seems that Scripture assumes that we know how to fill in the gaps. I've always found it interesting how little attention Isaac is given in the narrative of Genesis compared to his father Abraham and his sons Jacob and Esau. I read a midrash, once, a tiny fragment of a thought, in which the rabbis proposed that the silence of Isaac in the narrative is a reflection on his experience of being bound and nearly sacrificed. The rabbis reason that perhaps Isaac is just a bit quiet after that, keeps his head down, carries the burden of that moment with him for the rest of his life.

How factual this is, I'm not sure, but I appreciate the truth of the point.

Scripture is the story of God's redemptive action within and through and by humanity, and when the stories don't directly speak to that, it passes them by. It does not make the stories untold less important, but it does presume we can figure out the essentials, that even when not spoken of, people went on living, went on working out this haphazard way of faith, until God moved again and it was time to raise their heads or set their faces or go.

So I am offering the essentials here as a means to build a whole, a story that is about me but is really about God, and I trust that you can fill in the other bits. Your filling-in may not always be factual, but it may, in more ways than one, be true.

When I was in middle school, I had a moment, a flash—perhaps the voice of the Voice—when I believed that on her birthday my mother would be healed. I can't recall the evidence of this beyond my firm belief that I had heard something. I told everyone—my Sunday school teachers, my parents, my friends. Maybe there was part of me that secretly hoped I was a prophet of a kind. I don't put myself above that possibility. The day of her birthday I called my mother during a passing period in school and asked her if she had been healed yet.

"No." She said so carefully, with so much calm in her voice. My mother in the midst of all that pain is still one of the most gracious women I have ever known. I'm not sure how, except that she lives by a faith I can't contend with, a depth of trust that must take a lifetime to lay hold of. The rest of that day or the discussion that I am sure followed about discernment and wisdom and the difficulty in listening for God; all of that is a blur. What I remember is how this moment did not detour me from believing that God could speak. I had heard wrong, perhaps even fabricated what I had heard, but I was still convinced that God spoke and was always speaking in ordinary signs and wonders, sometimes in the quietness of the heart. So I began to forget. At some point I forgot to pray for the healing. At some point I forgot to believe it would come.

"Do you think she will be healed?"

Someone asks this at a party once, the kind of party with red cups and lukewarm soda.

"Yes."

Rote. I do not hear myself say it. I do not hear myself believe it.

My father believed in the power of books, which I think has everything to do with who I have become.

When I was in third grade he handed me Madeleine L'Engle's *A Wrinkle in Time*.

In eighth, Saint Augustine's *Confessions*.

In tenth, Margaret Atwood's *The Handmaid's Tale*.

And there were so many others. Countless others.

Months after handing me a book we would be driving somewhere and he would casually raise a theological question buried deep in one of the texts. We would end up spending an afternoon debating integrity or the Incarnation or sexual ethics or politics, all by telling stories, reading stories, and believing that the stories mattered.

I hand him books now. *Samsara*. The circles of our lives.

"To tell a story is an act of worship," he told me once, "To be entrusted with a story is an act of holiness."

We moved to Conroe, just north of Houston, the summer before I entered high school so that my father could become the director of missions for the local Baptist association. His new responsibility would be to serve as a pastor to pastors, connecting, encouraging, and resourcing over one hundred churches in the area. This made our Sundays a sliding scale of possibility. We joined a church that my mother and I could regularly attend, and my father would join us when he was able, but more often than not he was traveling somewhere, visiting a church in the association. Often I went with him. Small churches, big churches, cowboy churches and urban plants, white churches and black churches and multilingual churches. My father taught me the diversity within the faith by putting me in the center of it. I asked a lot of questions those days, driving back with him from a church. It was on those rides I learned that theology was contextual, that God cared about small groups of people as much as God cared about the whole.

"But how do we know we're right?"

"At some point, it has to be more about if we trust the Spirit of God," my father answered.

At some point. I've turned that over more times than I can count.

My spirituality in high school was complicated by an intense passion for the things of God and an intense desire to spend the majority of my summers hanging around a girl, making poor decisions that I am no longer proud of. Whatever I do or do not believe about sanctification, the refining of us into the image of God through the power of the Holy Spirit over time, I will say this: somehow in the midst of the infidelity of my heart, some rooted things took hold. I was not expecting to care about faith the way I seemed to. That was a surprise. I could be holding a well-emptied cup in the middle of the night, slouched on a kitchen counter, holding court about the beauty of Jesus and the glory of the cosmos. The incongruity of how that made me seem was not lost on me.

The church I joined was of the good sort, though its youth group was in a perpetual state of arrested development. Well-meaning adults with little formal Christian education attempted to lead high schoolers through the minefield of burgeoning philosophical inquiry. I asked all the dangerous questions in Sunday school. At least, I learned a year after I graduated high school and returned for a visit that they had been referred to as dangerous.

"But where did the angels come from? Did they just appear in the sky or did they travel from somewhere? Isn't Job the oldest book in the Bible and isn't there a strong case to be made that its roots are more myth than fact? Did you know the *Left Behind* books are heretical?"

This would have been an average Sunday. Three different youth leaders during their tenure at that church pulled me aside and asked me to go a bit easier on the volunteers.

"But shouldn't they know?"

This was always my response. Shouldn't the people who teach us about God know everything? Or, at least, shouldn't they be able to say that they don't know?

The one place where the dangerous questions could stand was at the kitchen table in our home.

During Sunday lunches I would lay out my theological concerns to my parents, and they would entertain them, tease them out. I would have to look things up or be expected to sit with something, to ask big and then have to think big. Some of the conversations we started then continue still. Evolution. Myth. Historical fact. Abortion.

"At some point, it has to be more about if we trust the Spirit of God."

I make my first international missionary journey the spring of my sophomore year in high school with my father. In an Eastern Orthodox church in Romania, we are followed by a witch muttering curses at our backs. She screams as if set aflame when we reach the icon of the Theotokos, Mary presenting the child Christ to the world. I am confused, because while I have felt the chill of unwelcome, I have not considered it the frost of evil.

"I could tell she was a witch."

My father says this, an hour later, a man who has never before spoken of this sort of thing. We are walking the burnt-auburn fields at twilight, discussing the places in the world where the old magic of demons still lingers.

"I began to pray against her when I felt her walk in. It seems like the Holy Spirit heard."

"Seems that Mary did too."

I think this. I do not say it.

I do not admit I have thought it, even to myself, until many years later, when I remember that Mary is the one who hears in silence. The space after the angel and Elizabeth. The timing of story in the Scripture. She sings a magnificat, then slips into the waiting. Yet within her? Light from Light.

"O Mary, bearer of Fire," Saint Catherine of Siena prays.

Would that we be like her. Would that I. I say this once to her face, in the middle of a church somewhere in Paris. She declines my words with her own silence. I light a candle, fire aligned with Fire, drop a coin in the box, and walk out of the church telling the Holy Ghost that I didn't know if she really could hear me or not and that the Spirit could sort it out.

I began skipping church for the first time my junior year of high school.

I would tell my parents I was going to the early service at church, but I'd really go to Starbucks or the café in the wealthier district that served a champagne brunch, where I'd write in a Moleskine and drink cappuccino. I would take a eucharist of croissant and cappuccino, tear the body and sip the blood. I would glide my pen across the pages and fill notebook after notebook with the certainties of my own importance. For a season, these notebooks and this bastard eucharist were my church. They were my means of grace. I wasn't disenchanted, I wasn't angry, but I was bored. Bored with the Baptist church that had been so good to me; bored with its smallness and its largeness.

My parents never found out directly. This detail, this period of lapsed attendance, was easily circumvented by what seemed to be harmless lies.

"What did you learn in church today?"

"That the world is charged with the grandeur of God."[16]

I learned this from the books I brought with me — N. T. Wright, Simone Weil, Kurt Vonnegut — and the notebooks. I learned this in the church of the champagne brunch. I learned this in the breaking of the croissant and the sipping of cappuccino.

I went on like this for a year and a half. Off and on. When I was a senior, before I left for college, a friend's bonfire was the perfect opportunity to set free that interim space. In an act of historical redaction, in an act of willing to write my past as something it was not, perhaps better, perhaps worse, I burned the notebooks. I burned the Moleskines. In a field in June when the moon hung so low the lake would have clapped its hands to touch it, I burned away that piece of self.

I met Meredith the summer before my senior year while on a mission trip to Mexico.

Riding around the back roads of a dusty town, we flirted shamelessly, stupidly, the way you only ever seem to be able to when you are young and careless, playing clumsily at language and virginity as if the two are interchangeable. Within a few weeks we were dating. Chaste, but silly-stupid in our emotions, falling for each other in that desperate way—when you think that all the songs you have ever heard echoing in slow dances are beginning to make sense, and you are willing to ignore the expiration date of youth, the futility of being intoxicated with another. I would always bring her flowers. She would always leave me notes.

We went on like that for months.

We were so sure of our affections that we found it easy to revise the history we were building as we were living it, to gloss over the instability of who we truly were. Meredith was the girl no boy could have at the small private school she attended, and I was the public school boy who had broken through. I had stolen her heart, and that ring of boys who had never been told no hated me for what I had managed to do.

Meredith liked this a bit too much.

Her pride in her unattainability meant that to hold her hand was to hold her down. She hated to be tethered, but hated more to be left, and we lived in a tension of my insecurity and her vanity. But we excused it between the two of us as the cost of a love too beautiful to be believed.

At least, this is what we told ourselves. Often. When we fought so loudly that the house across the lake turned its porch lights on. When she left me in the middle of the dance floor and slapped my hand away. When we pretended not to notice how sad we both were taking photos for our separate proms, because she had treated hers as the most important and I had done the same with mine.

I was the boy no girl had ever really dated, but who had made a few imperfect decisions with at parties or in hot tubs or on long bus rides late at night. My determination to get this relationship right, coupled with my insecurity that Meredith should one day wake up and see me as I was, dirty and arrogant, made me unfairly demanding of validation. I would feel wounded should she not praise me for the silliest of things and felt the fear of losing her whenever we sat on a bench near the lake in the middle of the night, talking about Kant and Joyce as if we knew what it meant to live or even to be.

We spoke of God the way we spoke of everything: far too certain and ridiculously malcontent.

We envisioned a world in which everyone was like us, wise to the ways of free spirituality, dangerous in thinking—dangerous in these days meant conceding that Roman Catholics might be Christians and it maybe wasn't a sin not to read your Bible every day. We let ourselves believe that we were like every great character in every great book, misunderstood by our time, lying on a bed of our own truth, thumbing our noses at the heavens and perhaps even at God.

We should have broken up maybe a half dozen times, but neither one of us wanted to admit defeat.

For our one year anniversary, I brought her back pearls from East Asia. They were cheap to buy there, of strangely good quality. I gave them to her out by the lake where we said that no one was ever like us or ever could be, eating a dinner on a picnic table covered in roses and surrounded by half-melted candles, because we were the sort of people who believed in pantomimed love.

The pearls meant something. The pearls meant we would get married. Somehow we both knew this. Somehow we both knew it would never be.

"They're beautiful. I'll keep them forever."

"Forever."

"You know what I mean."

"Yes."

"Yes."

And then she and I made out, so we didn't have to talk about it anymore.

⋈

Meredith and I both ended up going to Baylor University. She was planning on going somewhere else, a move in retrospect I realize was her attempt at a graceful bowing out. She wasn't even going to tell me, until I finally asked. A text message shattered my heart.

"I am going to ————. Don't hate me."

I drove over to her house in the middle of the night. I didn't bring her flowers.

"Baylor is a big place. Mer, if we break up, we'll be able to still go to the same university without it being weird."

"You think so?"

We are addressing the lake from the dock, not looking at each other.

"I know so."

"You don't. But I suppose it's pretty to think so."

Hemingway. I hate her and I love her in that moment.

The summer before I headed to Baylor, I traveled to a closed country in East Asia to serve as a missionary. Sort of.

I spent most of my time in coffee shops and trying local food. I ate fried scorpion and jellyfish salad, bought whatever looked the most surreal in the marketplace, and fell in love with the culture, the people, the ebb and flow of their lives.

"Give me an English name."

This is something that happens in this country often. Natives ask English speakers to give them English names of some significance. It becomes a seamless act of evangelism: give a biblical name, ask if they would like to hear where the name comes from, the story surrounding it.

Someone in our group gives her Mary. The girl is young, with patient eyes and the stance of a girl sure of only herself.

"What does this name mean?" she asks.

"She is someone who is very special to all of us," he explains. "Mary heard God."

"Mary heard an angel."

It slipped out of my mouth before I could bite it back.

"It's the same thing."

I only blinked at him and did not interrupt as he told the story, told about Jesus, told about hearing God.

"I want to hear God," Mary says.

"It's easy," he continues. "All you have to do is believe in Jesus."

All you have to do.

I come back to this scene often. I replay it. I pause it. I try and see myself and what expression I was making. I am still uncertain of how I should feel.

When I arrived at Baylor in August of 2008, within minutes of pulling boxes and bags into my dorm room in the Honors Residential College, I was herded into a tangle of other freshmen for a long weekend of forced bonding. Within an hour I hated everything about the experience. We were an amalgamation of awkward convictions, all of us Baptist, in an election year in the disputed territory of the Texan Christian. (Note the word order.) I foolishly pointed out there was a voting Democrat in their midst when the conversation turned to politics. As expected, someone immediately began talking about abortion. When I mentioned that it was possible to be a pro-life liberal, I was met with blank stares. I suggested we abort the conversation altogether to an impressively shocked circle of fellow eighteen-year-olds. I realized I was likely never to make friends here.

Meredith was supposed to be with another group, but she had tagged along because she had as much tolerance for the charade of forced community as I did. (She had voted Democrat in the caucus too, but had the good sense not to bring it up.) Otherwise, the only bright spot was Avery, a guy who had cracked a smile when I made the abortion pun. We both spoke uncomfortably to each other for the first hour, because we both falsely assumed the other was one of the leaders of the community charade. When we discovered that we were both the same age and both of the mind that the whole exercise was stupid, we became fast friends. We started talking about God, about our convictions for needing more depth in church; I was a good speaker and he played guitar, within a day we were already wondering what it would be like to start a church together. It felt true; truer than most things had felt in a long time.

The next day, I spent the afternoon doing laundry in the basement of my dorm. Being new to the environment and having been raised on film and television, I presumed that I needed to keep guard of the washing machine and drier at all cost. When I walked back upstairs with my clean clothes in tow, my phone erupted with missed calls that had not gone through while I didn't have cell service in the basement. Meredith and Avery had both tried three times. I called Mer, who told me that the aforementioned group had, as one of their activities, shared their testimonies for the past hour and a half.

If you are unfamiliar with sharing testimonies, its noble purpose is to communicate the unique story of God in a person's life, to offer encouragement, vulnerability, honesty; to proclaim where things have been, where things are. More often than not, however, the testimony circle, the sharing of one after the other, turns into a sin contest. Without fail, each person's story gets slightly worse than the one before. It is spiritualism telephone, because we have been led to believe that the worse we have been, the more God has forgiven us, the more impressive our story.

We say it's for the glory of God, but then again we say that about a lot of things.

Mer told me that it was incredible, rapturous, and about that time Avery knocked on my door, asked where I had been and if I wanted to hang out. We found Meredith and the three of us walked campus talking about the outbreaking of God during that time of honest, vulnerable sharing. The two of them were buzzing with excitement, certain it was a sign of something big.

I had missed out on the outpouring of the Spirit in the testimony circle.

This would become a running theme.

Three

CERTAINTY

THE NIGHT BEFORE THE start of term, all the students who lived in the Honors Residential College gathered in the Alexander Reading Room. We crammed across folding white chairs, encircling study tables, leaning against the walls, and sitting wherever there was room. Our headmaster, K. Sarah-Jane Murray, who I later came to call SJ, a fiery Irish woman who wore Vera Wang and quoted Ovid in Latin, stood firmly at the front behind a podium, a projection of the College crest beside her on a white screen.

"I challenge you: for what purpose have you come to this university?"

Her voice stretched out across the room, and everyone was transfixed. The portraiture on the walls seemed to strain to listen in.

"As members of College, you shall in your many courses encounter the works of Plato. Though it is doubtful, unless you take a course with me, that you shall encounter one of Plato's most significant works, the *Timaeus*. The *Timaeus* is oft forgotten. It does not contain the political argumentation of the *Republic* or the moral reasoning of *Euthyphro*, but it was nonetheless the most transcribed and commented upon philosophical text in the Middle Ages into the Renaissance."

She paused, held our gaze.

"It is perhaps for no reason but a mere one hundred lines, in which the myth of Atlantis is recounted. A relatively unremarkable tale as myths go: a civilization rises and falls. It was once, and then it is no more. Why bother, then, with its transmission? Why would the medieval scribes find it so fascinating?"

She smiled. What had been the projected crest of the College was replaced with a fragment of papyrus with Greek characters.

"On this fragment, the *Timaeus* tells us that the story of Atlantis has been shared as a reminder of what happens when things are not written down, preserved, and passed on. Atlantis had slipped into nothingness because no one bothered to recount the myth. The *Timaeus* is now atoning for that, bringing the myth back into the collective memory so that it might not be lost again. The medieval scribes took the point. Their own faith was one of stories. If the stories of the faith were not written down, the myths that shadowed the Christ who was to come and the tales of the followers who came after, then what would happen if one day there was no one left to tell the stories?"

The screen shifted back to the crest. "The motto of this College is taken from the twelfth-century theologian Saint Anselm of Canterbury: *fides quaerens intellectum*—'faith seeking understanding.' I ask you for what purpose you have come to this university. I hope that among the many answers you may give, this would be foremost among them: you have come to learn the old stories, the deep truths, the things into which angels long to look. You have come to take the texts of those who came before you and inscribe them on your hearts, to let them be the conversations that you dwell in. There are too many stories in this modern era that have fallen, like Atlantis, into the mists of forgotten things."

Her gaze set on each one of us, one after the other.

"Many of you have faith, but do you also have understanding? Do you have the storied perspective of the world that lets you participate in the grand drama? Generation after generation is entrusting the next with the collective memory of those who came before. Will you accept this task? Will you cherish it? Will you steward it well?"

She sent us out in silence.

During Christmas Vigil and Easter Vigil in liturgical churches, a significant portion of the service is given to a collection of several readings from the Bible. The stories weave together to tell a broad perspective of the plan of God's redemption from garden to resurrection.

I think of this as a gesture toward preserving the collective memory. We pass the stories on for the days when we forget, for the days when we are uncertain, for the middle-of-the-night moments when we think it impossible that God should be made man or that God should die and then rise again.

For the times of silence.

Do I steward it well? In the pause before the babe-cry that rings out of Bethlehem or the glory of the Lord that overtakes the soldiers at the empty tomb? In the breath-moment of terra uncertain. Do I hold on to the stories I have been given? Do I remember to pass them down?

Maybe that's what this is.

One of my best friends emailed me a few days ago about the Bible. He told me he thought that the reason why it was so cyclical, the same stories over and over again with different characters each time, was because the point was in remembering the feel of it. We retell the same stories so that we don't forget what it feels like to be a people wandering in the desert, searching for a promised land. We retell the same stories so that we don't forget what it feels like to be a people who were once called Not a People and have now been called by God.

I think of this as I try to write the past. I think of how I must have leached the emotion out of some fragments of the stories for the sake of being able to put them down. I am trying to remember how it felt to live them for the first time. Somehow I catch myself thinking of it like I think of Scripture, the cyclical retelling, and I marvel at how little we must change between the centuries, how in the end we're all still searching for a Kingdom that is not of this world, how we are so desperate to be known, to be called.

I entered Baylor determined to study political science. After my summer in East Asia and having grown up on Aaron Sorkin and NPR, I reasoned that even if I were to end up being a missionary someday a background in governmental affairs, particularly those of countries hostile to Christians, would be valuable. I paired this desire with one of Baylor's honors tracks, the Baylor Interdisciplinary Core, or BIC.

BIC is not a major in and of itself, but a humanities program that couples history, literature, the arts, science, and social theory into a four year, holistic survey of human anthropology from primordial age to present. It acts as the replacement for all common core requirements for majors in the College of Arts and Sciences. BIC is team taught, so you have a rotation of instructors and a combination of large group and small group discussion and lectures. It's an intensive program, but it can leave you wanting if you bend more toward literature, like I do.

A shorthand way of explaining BIC would be to say it's the track that doesn't read all the books. Because there is so much material to engage with and cover, BIC is unable to fit all of the reading into the courses that it would like to, so you end up reading only half of *The Odyssey* and supplementing the rest with summary, or you'll only read Dante's *Inferno* and skip over *Purgatorio* and *Paradiso* altogether.

Meredith chose BIC as well, majoring in history.

During the opening session of World Cultures I, the BIC history and literature intensive, a graying professor stood at the front of a room of two hundred largely evangelical college students and said, "Genesis is not the oldest historical account of the creation of the world."

Meredith and I made eyes at each other, incredulous. We were purists in the realm of heathens. We had heard stories of how these university types liked to belittle God and the Bible. We were prepared to confront them. We had a wall of certainty as our hedge of protection, firmly constructed around our hearts and minds.

I stopped listening. Because I disagreed with one part, I rejected the whole.

I was carefully religious in those opening days of class, determined to make college a marked point of transformation, a recommitment to the cause of Christ. I read my Bible daily and prayed purposefully. I asserted my Christianity with vigor and treated conversation as a circuitous dance that always led back to talking about Jesus. Cheaply, I could spiritualize anything and I did. There was a lot of talking about God in those days. There was a lot of piety bought on my own merits.

I was completely sure of what I believed, and I was terrified that no one would ever truly love me.

It makes a terribly mangled soul.

In the opening weeks of class, Meredith, Avery, and I formed a circle of friends we eventually called The Family. There was an artist and a girl Avery met during an orientation event, Addison, an artist herself, who came from the coast and smelled of the ocean. Mer and Addison grew close, around the same time that Avery and Addison picked up a relationship.

Soon after came Lexie, then two more, and April, all of whom had been in our welcome week group. The lot of us did nearly everything together. We ate meals together, studied together, cheered each other up, and told each other everything. We created a tradition of cooking together on Saturday.

(You do this in your first year of university, circling together like you'll never have friends again. You try and grasp hold of enough people to keep you afloat, enough signs that you will not end up alone.)

I had a dream, once, that we were all much older, by a decade or so, and we were dressed up for an event at which someone was receiving a biomedical award for contribution to the field. We walked up to a round table, hugging her before she walked up to accept. I told the group this, and they received it as a kind of prophetic possibility.

I didn't tell them that in the dream, Meredith wasn't the one beside me. I wasn't sure who was, but I knew it wasn't her.

This was how we played at spirituality. We put our faith in things like half-possible dreams and murmurs about God. We didn't do much by way of prayer and even less by way of Scripture, at least as a group. We floated on the traditions we were raised with and fed on the past. We prayed before our meals because it was the thing you were supposed to do.

We were the Israelites trying to take too much manna for one day, but we did not recognize it had not kept and were still eating from it, though it starved us.

.

⋈

Meredith and I fight all the time now. We fight because we don't know what else to do.

We see a movie one night and I don't hold her hand because the opening scene depicts a rape and I feel awkward reaching out to her in the midst of it. We walk and she doesn't speak to me, furious that I wouldn't touch her. We say all the things we promised we never would say.

We say all the things we should have said from the beginning. We forget that promises are not real unless they can be kept. We fall out of love and back into it so quickly we no longer know what it is to hate the other person or to love them. We make-out and she cries and I stiffen and we pretend it never happened. We do this a half dozen times before we start to notice, but even then neither of us points it out. We just pull grass from the patches of earth we sit on and watch it drift out of our hands.

If you are a student at Baylor, it is possible to go all four years of university and attend a different church every single Sunday while you are there. This is not an exaggeration. Waco boasts over a hundred Southern Baptist churches alone and a splintering baker's dozen of each Christian denomination otherwise.

The options for church are so numerous that a week into class, Baylor hosts a church fair on one of the campus malls where churches set up booths and pitch the different sorts of religious experiences they have to offer. You walk through a maze of overly excited clergy who have magnets with service times scrawled on them or little denominationally approved Bibles for you to add to your stack of free Bibles that as a recently graduated high school Christian you have an excess of. They offer to come pick you up and carpool you to services; they suggest that the church you went to back home wasn't as deep as they are. They ask if you want to go to church with David Crowder.

The Family walked around the booths and studied them incredulously. Lexie was a lapsed Roman Catholic, but enough of one that she wouldn't think of being anything else, so she found her circle quickly and rooted there. The rest of us were a mix of Baptist and nondenominational, so we drifted between options with the same sort of wide-eyed wonder that most people have when they first go to Disney World.

Promises were silently made that if you attended The Church of No Windows, you too would be cool enough to lazily throw around a Frisbee and talk about God in abstract statements that could double as Coldplay lyrics. Or you could attend The Church of the Flaming Spirit, which was, as its name suggests, a collective of college-aged students who believed that the only mode in which the Holy Spirit spoke through them was yelling, and who walked around campus asking people if they had a sister they could pray for, because they "had a feeling."

We went to The Church of the Flaming Spirit once, because they were said to have the best worship. It was a Wednesday night and The Family, minus Lexie, filed into one of the back rows of the large auditorium. After forty minutes of singing, hands lifted high, loud, thundering professions of lyrical faith, we were invited to sit while a member of the church came up to share his testimony. He wasn't more than twenty-five, an earnestness in his face that I've rarely seen on someone so young. He told us about being incredibly high one night at a party when he was suddenly convicted by the Holy Spirit that he needed Jesus.

Meredith twitched beside me. It sounded like a Ben Folds song.

He began to tear up, recounting the moment he triumphantly surrendered to Jesus and asked him to come into his heart.

"And then," he rasped into the microphone, "and then I felt this wind blow into my side. This huge rush."

Some people in the audience began to clap, a few began to stand and jump up and down. "And *he* came into me, y'all!"

There was cheering, loud and raucous.

"And then I felt another wind against my other side!"

More cheering.

"And I knew *he* was in me!"

That's when I stood. I stood, looked at Meredith, then at Avery, who was on my other side, and said, "I'll be in the car." And I walked out.

In retrospect, I am not entirely sure why I left. When The Family came out after the service, I said it was something to do with the two rushes of wind.

"Why does the Holy Spirit need two rushes of wind?" I asked incredulously. "Wasn't one enough?"

If this sounds hollow to you, it's because it was. Even now, I don't have a satisfactory explanation for my reason, but I can tell you that I never went back to The Church of the Flaming Spirit, and I was never tempted to. Talking about God like this made me tense all over. Maybe I wanted the experience described but was ashamed to admit I had never felt it. Maybe I thought I had the good sense to see it as nothing more than sensationalism. Maybe, I'm not sure.

A few years ago, on a breezy April eve, two members from The Church of the Flaming Spirit approached me on campus and asked if I was a Christian. When I told them I was, they asked what kind. (In Waco, this is not a strange question.) When I said that I was sort of Baptist and sort of Episcopalian, they suggested that while that was all right, it was like I was going on a camping trip with God and that I had insufficient equipment. I was going with a ratty old sleeping bag. If I wanted the right equipment, like a new sleeping bag, I would really need to go to their church.

I opened my mouth to retort rather viciously, but then I felt a rush of wind push against one side of me. A moment later, a rush of wind brushed against the other. I shut my mouth, turned away from them, and kept walking toward the library.

"Funny," I whispered to the wind.

The wind did not reply.

Most nights, Avery and I would stay up late in the hallway of our dorm talking. We turned over everything, at least what we believed to be everything. We laid out our grievances with the church and the lack of care it had for our generation. We hungered for a faith experience that owned fully the power of God but didn't cheapen itself into mere feelings. We made passing half-jokes about our earlier thoughts of one day starting a church together.

He was still dating Addison then, and we made our friendship out of a sense of superiority. We were a little bit ahead of the others in The Family, already in romantic relationships, driven by our ambition to do something with our lives, clever enough not to have to work particularly hard when it came to school. Avery liked that I had ideas; I liked that he could follow them. He was also, for lack of a better word, the coolest person I had ever known. Being friends with him was an ego boost that I had never experienced before.

He was my best friend. Somewhere along the way, it happened, and since I had never had a best friend before, I clung to it the way I had clung to my certainty about God: possessive and cripplingly self-conscious.

In our attempts to make spiritual spaces where there was already an overwhelming amount of them, Avery and I led The Family to begin a Bible study that met on Thursday nights at 9:42 in the evening for reasons that now escape me.

9:42 started out as a study through a book of the Bible, like James. Only Avery or I led it, because no one else felt comfortable doing it or perhaps no one else felt brave enough to challenge us.

We averaged about fifteen or so people, sitting on the floor of the Memorial classroom on the first floor of the girls' dorm in the College. The studies were simple, direct, and without much conviction.

There was one time when Addison brought a friend from class, and he turned out to be a staunch Calvinist. He and I ended up fighting about free will for two hours. I felt it my duty to defend God. He never came back, which I thought was for the best, because it was bad enough that he was a Calvinist, but God forbid he corrupt anyone else in the group.

In a notebook I came across recently, I had scrawled down something about 9:42, James 2, and faith without works being dead. The Bible study group was an attempt to move us from a faith that did not have works into a faith that did, though the truth that it was just another hour to spend chatting around God as opposed to genuinely reaching out to God did not seem to occur to us.

Wait. I take that back.

Once, Addison baked chocolate chip cookies and had us go with her around to the apartments near campus that were occupied by some of the poorest people in Waco. We offered cookies to every person we met, an action that was often seen as ridiculous. No one was particularly impressed with the gesture, but we did it all the same. We thought this was acting out faith. I suppose it was. How does anyone really measure that sort of thing, anyway?

We are sitting on the front porch of the College, chairs turned out and legs on the stone railing.

Chris, a mess of brown curls, is the wife of the College chaplain, and we've been slow friends for the past few months. We drop one-liners of theological maybes between us and see if the other decides to pick them up. We determine whether or not we'll have an extended discussion from that. Chris is studying at Truett, the seminary affiliated with Baylor, and she feels called to be a pastor.

I am certain about what I believe about these things. I have my prepared answers. I have my fixed feelings.

"So if the Holy Spirit speaks into my heart and says that I am called to this, you think I'm just making it up?"

She is not accusatory. Chris is remarkable this way. She speaks conviction slow, careful, just enough to prick your soul without puncturing you to the point of hemorrhage.

"Maybe you misheard."

"Ah."

She breathes, surveys the landscape of people changing classes in front of us, the scuffle to chapel and the dining halls, the bohemian transients in flowing dresses stretched out on blankets reading Thoreau.

"How are you so sure that you hear the Holy Spirit more clearly than I do?"

I have told her about my own calling, years ago, to be a missionary. This is the first time she has addressed it directly.

"Because I don't want the call and usually that's a sign it's God."

Chris nods slightly, kicks her legs off the stone, and smiles.

"Yeah," she says sarcastically, "I really wanted to be called to preach in a world where my own people resent me for it."

She tosses her hair and grabs her bag.

"I have to head to class."

Chris turns and takes a half step before turning back.

"You know so much more than you know, Preston Yancey, but you know so much less than you think you do."

One night before 9:42, The Family was sitting in a communal study space, picking through that night's homework when someone raised the question of women being pastors. Avery and I spoke a lot, spoke with a great amount of conviction, and guarded our staunch belief against them with a fierce sense of pride. April clutched at the cross around her neck the entire time before she stood and walked out, shouting a few angry things over her shoulder as she left. Addison and Mer rose to go after her, but she told them to stay. A few minutes later, the girls went ahead and went downstairs to the classroom for the Bible study while the boys lingered a bit longer. A few more words were exchanged, shifting the blame for April's reaction around. When we made to go downstairs ourselves, I felt a flame settle over me and I stopped.

Avery looked back at me.

"Are you coming?"

"No," I heard myself say, "I'm going to go talk to April."

He looked at me then with such contempt. They left me to gather my things, which I did slowly, packing my Bible into my bag and walking empty handed down the stairs and outside to the front porch of the building, where April sat at a patio table looking up at the stars.

"I'm sorry" was the first thing I said. I wasn't entirely sure for what I was apologizing, for my belief or for my delivery. The words clung to the space between us and after a moment I sat down across from her.

April said nothing for a long time, fingering the cross around her neck until she finally spoke.

"I'm not a Christian."

I blinked at her.

"I wear this cross around my neck so you all will not talk to me about it, so I can just get by."

She shook her head and dropped it from her fingers.

"But I don't believe any of it, Preston. I want to, but I don't."

Our words were slow for the next hour, metered out with a care that I can only describe as supernatural. I have rarely followed the usual rubric for talking to people about Jesus, about saying a little prayer and hoping something sticks. But on that porch with April, I found myself repeating over and over again that God was a God of unfailing love, that she was seen, that she was known, and at some point my arms were around her as she cried for a pain as old as the cosmos, and she asked me how to pray. I led her simply, phrase by phrase, and when we reached "amen" together, April stopped crying and leaned back in her chair, wide-eyed and staring at me.

"I feel it," she gasped, pointing to her chest, "I feel peace."

I began to cry, because God was real and I had forgotten, more than once, but in April's amazed eyes I saw again.

When we walked back into the classroom, 9:42 was wrapping up, and April carefully told everyone what had happened.

We went out for food after that, at a twenty-four-hour pancake house where we told them it was April's birthday and they brought her chocolate chip pancakes with whipped cream. It was true enough. It was beautiful and loud and impossibly light.

It was around that same time that Avery and I were in our dorm after one of The Family's Saturday night meals when he looked over at me and asked calmly, "What do you think about starting a church?"

I was still holding the large, dirtied bowl I had used to make a trifle that was a combination of brownies, whipped cream, and toffee that I had called Sin.

"What?" I feigned surprise, but I knew exactly what he was talking about.

The thought of starting a church, truly starting a church, had been pooling in my spirit for days, ever since April's conversion. The idea knocked around my mental furniture and demanded to be accounted for until I had all but stifled it as a reaction to the exciting news and nothing more, and then came Avery's question.

He was looking at me in that serious way he had. He could read my face and knew I wasn't exactly handing over all I had to offer. For all the times I worried about screwing up our friendship, I missed in the process how much he actually did love me, how he read me sometimes better than Meredith did, and how he did, completely, care. I would forget that again, but in that moment I was completely aware of it.

"I've thought about it." I said weakly, just loud enough that it took up the smallest space between us.

After another moment, we parted ways, with me saying no repeatedly as I walked down the hall away from him. It was ridiculous, absurd.

In my own room, I set the dirtied bowl on top of my dresser and reached for my Bible, doing the one thing I had forsworn never to do again after those days of church camp. I opened and threw down my finger and read the verse I landed on.

Look among the nations, and see; wonder and be astounded. For I am doing a work in your days that you would not believe if told.[1]

I felt sick to my stomach. I texted Avery: "I think we're supposed to do it."

A minute later he replied, "Me too."

We told Meredith and Addison the next day. Mer only nodded and Addison said, "Absolutely. This is the work of God."

At the next meeting of 9:42, we laid out a strategy for what it would look like. We pictured a Saturday night college service that would be just like a Sunday morning service, only uniquely tailored for a university crowd.

I carefully told The Family that God had laid on our hearts a direction, a movement for Baylor, that was rooted in the stories of looking after those who had been forgotten. Like the Samaritan woman in John 4, we would offer living water to those who did not feel that they had a place in the Church. We'd call it The Well.

There is a rash of weekends and more than one weeknight when we pile into cars and drive to Austin, about an hour and a half from Waco.

None of us are old enough to drink, so we just go to go, walking around the city and eating from food trucks, seeing movies, running around the grounds of the capitol.

We play a game called Truth, which was originally Truth or Dare until no one would pick dare and we were left with nothing but the tangled questions we used to learn from one another.

It is a game that lends itself to cruelty. More than once.

"If you had to date someone beside Addison, who would it be?"

Someone asks this of Avery.

"Meredith."

It comes quickly, not too quickly, but it comes fast. He pulls me aside later to make sure I was all right with his answer, and I tell him that I am. And I was. Mostly.

We are young and we are foolish and we believe that nothing will destroy us and that words have no power but what we give them. We believe we are the most interesting people ever to have lived. We believe that we are pioneers of a new sort of freedom and acceptance. We are children playing with oldest fire, speeding down the highway in the middle of the night, driving from darkness to darkness in want of light without Light.

During one of these trips, Addison and Avery break up. They stay friends, but we all feel it, textured in the darkness, how our grasping for commonality and security isn't as sure as we hope. I tell Avery I'm on his side. He tells me there are no sides.

There are, but I don't correct him.

My father advised Avery and me to partner with an established church that would allow us to base our ministry idea from within it, as opposed to just going at it on our own. We begrudgingly accepted the wisdom of this, though we were not subtle in how it made us feel constrained.

We spent months trying to find a church that would sponsor The Well. We came close a few times, but it always fell apart by the time we were about to follow through.

We weren't shy about our ambitions. We would meet for weekly coffees to plan, which we called staff meetings. We made email signatures that announced us as co-pastors of The Well. We had Addison draw up sketches of a possible logo. We started a Facebook page. We told professors that we would not be able to make certain events because we were responsible for a church.

Somewhere in this we stopped praying. I am uncertain of when, but it happened.

Avery and I liked to joke that we were the sons of thunder from the Gospels, James and John. We thought that meant we were given the power to call down fire from heaven and believed that was in and of itself a sort of perpetual holiness. So we stopped trying. We were God's anointed and these were the days of awe. What else did we need?

It's sometime in November. We are sitting on the giant mall that faces the library, the field cut low and a blanket spread beneath us. Meredith and I do this often. We pick up sometime after midnight and go somewhere on campus just to be. Our communal life, the habit of clustering you form in that first year away from home, becomes suffocating. This is our way of breaking free.

There is the time we explore the fountain tunnels that run below the science building; the time we sneak up the bell tower; the time we climb the oldest oak, branches wide enough to share.

Tonight we are in the clearing, in the crisp grass, lying on a blanket and charting the canopy of the cosmos, making silent promises neither of us could ever be expected to keep.

She is not touching me, but I can feel her. The space between our forearms, the electricity of proximity, the almost touch, like her soul is stretching out, trying to make contact with my own.

"I don't hear God the way you and Avery do."

Her words rupture the air above us, a chipping of the spiritual firmament.

"What do you mean?"

"When you both say you *feel* God telling you to do something, I don't understand it."

I don't look over to her, but I can hear her dragging her finger beneath the pearls around her neck, the tap of them against her flesh. Though she has never said this aloud, I believe she hates necklaces. I believe she hates them because they are too much like a leash.

"I was never taught to listen for that. I know what it's like to feel passionate about Jesus, but I don't know what you mean when you say you hear him."

I don't speak for a long time. A wind, like the wind over the chaos of the waters in Genesis, slips over and between us.

"What's it like?"

"It's not audible. It's not words exactly. It's like your heart is pulling out toward some direction, like it's trying to get there before you can, and it's trying to tell you to keep up. I think that's the Spirit."

We don't say anything else and eventually we fall asleep. Around four in the morning, I wake to find Meredith gone. The blanket still holds the impression of her body, and for a moment I believe she has left for good. When I glance behind me, I see her: halfway up the mall, back to me, looking at the stars. There's a chill settling in, so I wrap the blanket around me as I walk over to her.

"Mer? What's up?"

She doesn't turn to me.

"I don't know."

And, after a moment, "I just don't know anymore."

On our year and a half anniversary, I give Meredith a ring made of a simple gold band and two black pearls, which I bought while I was in East Asia. It is a little surprise, a small trail of candles and clues across campus to a field, which Addison helps me set up. It isn't an engagement ring or even a promise ring, but something romantic and yet something empty.

She receives it hollowly, but she masks herself just enough to seem appreciative.

"She told me it terrified her. She knew in that moment she would never marry you and she couldn't figure out how to tell you without losing a piece of herself in the process."

Addison tells me that a year later, when we are walking by the spot where I had given Meredith the ring.

There is nothing special about the spot, except that it has now been written down. It has now been ensured not to be forgotten. It is being passed down. Though whether or not it's important to pass it down, I'm not so sure.

"Did you want to marry her?" she asks me, her hand entwining with mine.

"No."

"I knew."

"I know."

It seems so long ago.

We keep vigil in that place for a moment, then keep walking.

I have lost track of the exact spot in that field. Maybe that's for the best.

During Dead Week in December, the days set aside between the end of term and the start of exams, I spent most of my time studying without a lot of focus. My notes were haphazard, my attention splintered by the tenuous ground Meredith and I were occupying and the uncertainty of The Well and its future.

I had a spiritual journal due for one of the courses of BIC that I have recently forced myself to reread. The arrogance of it turns my stomach. It drips with certainty, with the polished ivory tower elitism of a faith that has never had to account for itself fully. The last line, now, does me in:

I arrived at this from the peace that surpasses all under-standing. Trying to explain it is hopeless. If you have it, you know what it feels like. It's as simple as that.

As simple as that.

The day before exams, I woke up with a wild idea to go home. I grabbed my bag and got in my car and drove the two and a half hours, Bright Eyes and The Swell Season blasting the whole way.

My parents didn't quite know what to do with me showing up like that. They were concerned about me driving back later that night. It was supposed to ice and the roads might close. I was inexperienced on that stretch of roadway, easily distracted in the dark. There wasn't much that could be done, though, with a 9:00 a.m. French exam the next morning, so they conceded that I could return that evening.

I spent the day at my old high school, chatting with my former AP European and World History teacher, working through my World Political Systems study guide for the final. She helped me put my thoughts in a sort of order, and I was grateful for the time. But in fairness, it wasn't exactly beneficial.

I point this out by way of retrospect. I point this out, because I am realizing the point was not that I had come home to study for my finals.

I stayed through dinner. It had been by chance, but my paternal grandparents were there, my grandfather still receiving chemotherapy from MD Anderson in Houston. He was the sickest I had ever seen him. At our dining room table that night, he was a shade of himself. We ate in quiet. We ate around the edges of the thing none of us would say out loud. I hugged him. I kissed his cheek. I left as quickly as I had come.

I drove back in the dark. North of Huntsville, in the space where the city meets the untamed landscape, I hit a patch of ice and my car slid hard to the right. I felt the movement like in a dream, my body pulled before my mind followed, foot slowly pulling off the gas, slowly touching the brake, hands on their own accord holding the wheel with care. Behind me, I saw headlights flash as a car pitched up and off the side of the road into the ditch. There was the sound of a crash, of chaos, and just as quickly the flash of more lights, a highway patrolman behind us. I found myself back in the lane. Safe. Only briefly shaken. I was waved on by the patrolman. I am not sure what happened to the car behind me. The rest of the drive is a blur.

I arrived back at campus in time to meet up with Meredith, Avery, and the rest at Common Grounds, the coffee shop near campus, to hear a friend play a set at the last open mic night of the semester.

"How was home?" Meredith whispered, taking my hand and leaning into me.

"Fine." I murmured. I didn't say anything about the car, about the flash of lights, about what had nearly happened.

That day was the last time I saw my grandfather alive. He passed away a week later.

It was a beautiful funeral, if these things can be called beautiful.

I remember my father at the front of the church giving the sermon.

I remember Meredith beside me.

I remember not crying.

I remember going back to *their* house and stopping myself and calling it *her* house because it was now just *her* house, and I remember that being the point that I felt it most.

Meredith left a few hours afterward to drive back home. This had impressed my parents—because she had showed up.

I didn't tell them that I had had to tell her to, that I had had to call her and tell her she should come.

I knew then, but I also didn't.

Christmas was and then wasn't. I have consulted my calendar and find nothing written there.

I have to presume it happened, but I can find no evidence.

What happens when things are not written down?

Like that field. Like the readings for Christmas and Easter. Like Atlantis.

Four

---·---

FRACTURES

WHEN TERM RESUMED IN January 2009, Sarah-Jane emailed me a brief invitation to come sit in on her survey of ancient literature, which she taught as an introductory course in the Great Texts program, a major devoted to studying the literary tradition of Western civilization.

Over the course of the previous semester, I had chatted with her off and on after lectures and at afternoon coffees hosted by the College about the tension I felt in BIC, not reading the whole book and moving so quickly from text to text I felt only a passing familiarity with its existence, let alone its meaning. Her invitation was an attempt to remedy that.

One early January morning, I trudged down to the bottom floor of my dorm to one of the classrooms in the College and sat in the back of a room of fifteen other students with a copy of the *Timaeus*. Sarah-Jane entered five minutes late, asking why none of us had bothered to use the first five minutes to chat about the reading we had been assigned and to get to know one another so that we had people to study with.

Being five minutes late was part of her plan. I would come to learn, quickly, that everything Sarah-Jane did was part of a plan.

A few weeks into the course, I had fallen in love with her way of reading books, which I quickly learned was the policy of the Great Texts department as a whole. We moved slowly, carefully. We had to own the perspective of the work we were holding and had to critique only in so far as the text allowed us to. We were not looking for universal truths or sweeping statements, but a judicious assessment of what exactly this particular people from this particular time in this particular place were offering to us. And we read the whole book.

At one point, I think while we were in the middle of Homer, I mentioned to Sarah-Jane that I was considering writing my undergraduate thesis on interpreting Virgil's *Aeneid* as a treatise against Roman authoritarianism and exceptionalism. She studied me incredulously.

"Maybe."

That was all she offered.

The next class, Sarah-Jane pulled me aside at the end and put a thin book into my hands.

"These are the short stories of a supposed French woman we call Marie de France. She lived in the twelfth century. Go read these and then come back and tell me if you still want to work on Virgil."

I read the book in two days.

In her opening lines, Marie's scribe instructs the reader:

> It was customary for the ancients, in the books which they wrote ... to express themselves very obscurely so that those in later generations ... could provide a gloss for the text and put the finishing touches to their meaning.[18]

"I'm switching my major." I called my parents the day I finished the last story. "I'm dropping BIC and changing to Great Texts as my major and Political Science as my minor."

They were hesitant. They needed time to pray. I had Sarah-Jane call them. A few minutes in, they mentioned they had already arrived at a place of peace.

"You have good parents," Sarah-Jane offered. "Most of the time parents want for their children what they never had. That's usually money."

She smiled warmly.

"There's no money in studying books."

She jerked her thumb up toward the sky.

"But I think there's something of riches up there with the Big Guy."

I just nodded.

"Sure."

With the Big Guy.

Addison didn't come back for the spring semester. The reasons were unclear.

Meredith cried for a day when we found out the news.

"I'm so alone now."

She said that outside her dorm, in the dark.

I didn't say anything in reply. I only nodded.

She was.

Someone tells us about a church in the north part of Waco that might be interested in partnering with us. It doesn't have a website, doesn't even have a phone number listed, so Avery and I plan on driving over Sunday morning and are just hoping we manage to show up on time for church.

We are sitting up in the communal kitchen of the girls' dorm, another Family dinner, and in the aftermath exchanging stories about possibilities, about a church that may someday be. Meredith sits across from me at a table, angled close to someone else, the two of them whispering about something I can't quite catch. They've looked over at me a few times.

I can't understand what Meredith needs. It hangs between us.

A few days ago Meredith and I went for frozen custard and sat under the halogen lights, counting the reasons why we would stay together. So much of it was about expectation. Maybe it was about letting her stay. Our frozen custard melted before either of us had taken a bite. We threw them away as a homeless woman walked past asking for change. We had spent the last of it on the custard.

April is knitting. Her yarn is a tangle of blue, pink, lime green. Someone describes it as "Easter vomit" and she is not embellishing, but I soften it by calling it "cotton candy." April is attempting socks or perhaps a scarf, something that has consumed her for the past hour while telling a story about going to a megachurch when she was growing up in the country and would have to drive forty-five minutes with her family into *town*, as she put it.

"There was a laser show at Christmas."

"Awesome!" Avery grins.

I blink at him. It is like I am seeing him for the first time. I am about to say something but am distracted by a question, and by the time I would be able to speak to it again, the moment has passed. We are talking about something else, something that he teases me about by saying that if I am not careful, he will build our church with stained glass that looks like April's yarn.

The point is not the color; the point is the stained glass. It is too old, too other, too *that kind* of Christian. I hold back the part of me that wants to confess I like stained glass, because I can feel the dividing of us even then. I can hear the warning that if I'm not careful, something will happen.

That night, I lie awake in my bed like it's Christmas Eve, unable to sleep. There is nothing to be excited about, at least nothing that comes immediately to mind. The church may or may not be what we need, it may or may not be the answer. Perhaps I'm excited. Perhaps I know what is coming. Perhaps I am consumed with thoughts about Meredith and Avery, about the fear of being abandoned, about holding on desperately so that I won't have to be alone in the dark in the middle of the night unable to sleep.

Avery and I spend most of the next morning unable to find the church. We drive around for an hour and keep missing it, ending up on the other side of town, ready to give up. We nearly do, until one last pass and we round a corner to see a massive Baptist steeple in the middle of a rundown neighborhood, the church's name in crooked letters on the side of the disheveled building.

We park, take tentative steps out, and see a rotund man standing at the door of the smaller building beside the larger. He waves us over, welcomes us, tells us he is Pastor Joe and he's excited to have us worshiping with them that day. We have arrived, apparently, right as they are about to begin.

It's a small chapel. About thirteen pews on either side. There are bars on the windows. The carpet it burgundy, loud and red, and it smells of wilted lilies and Lysol. There are about twenty people in attendance, most of them women, and none of them younger than sixty. A woman at the front is at the electronic piano. She begins the hymn, and Avery and I are passed hymnals with a sort of awe. The whole thing is a dream, and I sit wide-eyed throughout the service while Avery weeps.

"Can we talk with you a moment?"

One of us asks this when the service is over, and Pastor Joe takes us back to his office. We tell him our story, what we have been looking for and looking to do. We tell him that this place feels like home, feels like where we're supposed to be, and when it's all been told, when all the words have been placed out in whatever order we managed to untangle them into, he looks at us with tears in his own eyes.

"I have been praying every day for a year that God would do a work in this place to bring life back to it. I have been praying for someone young to walk through those doors. Today, I was about to announce this would be my last Sunday at this church, but God whispered, 'Wait.' "

He smiles broadly; he swallows.

"And then you all show up."

Now I cry. Soft. Careful. I look around his office, at his picture of a 1970s white Jesus, at the wood paneling, and realize I am home.

Joe asks if we want to see "the church where you will be serving," and we say yes. He takes us around the chapel, then outside to the larger building.

"This used to be the sanctuary. This church used to run over two thousand people on a Sunday. Who knows, maybe that's what you're both here to do."

Avery and I smile at each other and walk inside.

We are telling Joe about the idea of Saturday night services, about being laid back and simple. He just keeps nodding, so we keep talking.

In the foyer there is a row of photos on the wall of the former pastors. As Joe leads Avery into the sanctuary, I stay behind and look. All men, all white, all earnest. I can see calling tinged in their eyes, though perhaps there is an agedness to them after each photo, as if each new pastor had known this particular church was slipping away. What had they endured? What had they seen?

"Preston, you need to come see this!" Avery calls me, surprised, and I turn and quickly make my way to him, pushing open the door and then stopping short.

We are standing in an empty church sanctuary, a sanctuary that has once seated two thousand, bathed in the darkness of no lights save what streaked through its windows.

The windows.

They are cotton-candy stained glass. Swirling colors.

The color of April's yarn.

Meredith and I break up in the side hallway of her dormitory. It's after we have sat through a performance by something from Vivaldi. I feel nauseated beside her the entire time, and when we are back at the dorm I ask her if we can talk. After two hours of tears and anger and revisited wounds, we issue a joint text message to The Family.

Avery calls me. "I'm sorry, man. Hope we can all still be friends."

I take four Benadryl and pass out watching *The West Wing*.

When I wake the next morning, Meredith has sent me a text: "Do you want the ring back?"

I don't reply. She doesn't press the question.

I have been rereading the messages between Meredith and me.

I have been arranging them on a table like evidence.

I have been fitting the pieces together to try and tell it as true as I can, to be neither too gracious nor too harsh, to tell only the portion of the story that is really mine to tell.

What if you wanted it to end or thought it should? If that were true and I realized it would only hurt you to keep

*on, then of course I would walk away, I wouldn't be able
to say that I love you and not do that. So yes, I have an
absolute: I know that I love you and I know that barring
the necessity for your sake, I will not leave you.*

One of us wrote that to the other.

With all the exchanges laid out like this, I wonder how I
missed it.

I wonder how I missed how terribly sad we both were.

"I know so."

"You don't. But I suppose it's pretty to think so."

Over sixty people attended the first service of The Well.

A mixture of students and adults, we crammed into the small
chapel on a Saturday night in late January. The whole Family was
there, except Addison, whom we had pray for us in the service over
speakerphone. Avery led the music. I preached a sermon about the
woman at the well in John 4.

I explained that we were called The Well because it was the place
anyone could come and drink, anyone could come and meet Jesus.
I probably spoke too long, I tend to do that, but by the time it was
over, there was hugging and excitement and a buzz of possibility.

People wanted to know about the plans for the future, about
what we thought it could be. I said something about trying to bring
revival to Baylor.

Revival.

One little word can mean all that. I pushed it out of me because
I didn't want it myself, under the gaze of a framed holographic
Jesus on the back wall that someone had put up in the chapel in the
1960s and never bothered to take down. He followed you as you
moved, and though it was tacky and vulgar, it was also a reminder
of something true.

Antonia was there. She was full of light even then, but I didn't know how to see it. Antonia, whom I knew then only from half-conversations in class and editing a few papers, walked up and gave me a soft hug and said she enjoyed it. I think the look she gave me then was something of sadness. She knew how to hear the flesh beneath the spirit.

I thanked her for coming. I was so proud of it. So proud of us, what we had accomplished. I was proud that we had done something for Jesus, while the holographic Jesus paced behind Antonia's head, silently wondering when I would look up and consider him.

Meredith slipped up to me, as people were leaving.

"This is good. It will be good."

"Thank you."

She hugged me.

We never touched each other again.

It happens slowly, the way it becomes about us and not about God. It happens when we change our email signatures to include that we are pastors, when we sit a little straighter in our chairs when we talk about the Bible, when we look at people like they should defer to us because we are the ones who know.

We aren't a Family anymore. We are two people and those other people. We are us and they are them.

It happens before you realize it has happened.

It happens the moment you believe that your spirituality has surpassed that of someone else, that you can be their Holy Spirit.[19]

Avery and I met Isabelle and her best friend, Celia, at Common Grounds one Friday afternoon in early February. They wanted to know about The Well. They had ideas about how to partner with a neighboring elementary school to start a backpack program that would provide poor students with backpacks full of school supplies and food. We chatted for about an hour, figuring out the logistics and the structuring of a nonprofit ministry, and by the time we were getting up to leave I had already seen it. It was an exchange between Isabelle and Avery, the way he tipped his cup toward her just once and she smiled into the corners of her mouth and tilted her head to one side.

"So Isabelle," I began that night when Avery and I went driving around, windows open, feeling Texas winter on our skin.

"Yeah," he beamed, "Yeah. Isabelle."

I wanted to tell him to be careful, but I didn't know why, so I didn't. I was still raw from Meredith, the prick of the dissolution had deflated parts of me I didn't know she had been supporting.

The night was blue, even then, even that late. It was winter and the night was still blue. I stared up into it while I drank a chocolate-and-banana frozen something and we sped down the part of the highway the police never watched.

"It's good to see you happy again, man," Avery looked over at me, nearly shouting as the wind ripped through us.

Blue nights. We lived our lives in blue nights.

"I'm happy for you," I replied.

I suppose we both had missed the point.

I wouldn't officially leave the BIC program until the end of the semester. In order for the classes not to have been a waste, I needed to stick with it to the end of the first year and then have the classes transfer over for equivalency in my new degree program in Great Texts.

It was during this time that I met Professor Constance Harmon, who taught my small group module in World Cultures II. Professor

Harmon was mysterious, whimsical. She likened herself to Demeter, goddess of the harvest, growing in her students the seeds of learning she scattered wild and free. She not only demanded excellence but also expected cleverness. We would sit in class and ask a lot of *why* questions when it came to history and very little *what*. Days we were supposed to be talking about indigenous tribes in the Americas or early Islamic philosophical engagement turned quickly into dialogues about colonization as theory of ideological practice and whether or not it still went on today, carefully masked, under the premise of social progress from a small intellectual elite that was really after monopolizing control.

We never fully understood what she was talking about, which seemed to suit her just fine. She would pose these massive questions, eyes aflame, and be pleased when we left with more uncertainty than we had entered with.

"But never," she told us once, "leave here disbelieving what you believe is true. Question it. Wrestle with it. But never believe that because I said something, it's gospel."

She winked at us.

"There is but one gospel."

I didn't quite believe her. The way she talked, I was pretty sure she wasn't a Christian. She was too liberal. She was too loud. She was too certain of how uncertain the world was. I distrusted her.

"Dr. Harmon, I can't go on the field trip to the mosque on Saturday, I'm supposed to be preaching."

I tell her this outside of class once.

"Call me Constance. Find someone to guest preach," she said simply, "or fail." And she walked off.

I found someone to guest preach.

We walked around the mosque that Saturday, told we were being exposed to Islamic culture. Constance came up beside me, quietly.

"This isn't a mosque."

87

She said it carefully,

"The people here are too rich. They are too caught up in the show of all of it. This is supposed to be a house of prayer."

And she walked away, gingerly, peeking around others and murmuring something else to them. I think on it now and imagine she was trying to tell each of us what she thought we needed to hear.

This is supposed to be a house of prayer.

April was baptized by Joe in the old baptismal of the abandoned sanctuary, light slipping through the cotton-candy stained glass. The Family was there, along with a handful of others.

Lexie skipped Mass to be there for it, and when Pastor Joe baptized April in the name of the Father, the Son, and the Holy Spirit, Lexie made the sign of the cross upon herself.

I watched her, bathed in blue-pink light, and something in me, something quiet, broke lose when she made that sign. While everyone clapped, someone shouted, someone cheered, I kept staring at the hand Lexie had used to cross herself. I kept wondering about bodies and prayer. I kept wondering if somewhere along the way, I had missed something.

I am not sure what I did for Holy Week that year.

I have marked on my calendar *EASTER BREAK* across a four-day period beginning Good Friday and ending Holy Monday.

I remember that Avery was supposed to come home with me for the break.

"Isabelle's family invited me over. It would be really good to spend this time with them."

"Of course. I understand."

I didn't. I still don't. And yet I do.

⋈

This all seems such a waste. Starting a church. I suppose much of it was, in a way, but there were moments of good.

There was the time the guy who was visiting from another school came to The Well and asked if I would pray for him, who kept in touch for a year, who reached out again and again as he struggle-questioned his way toward Home.

There was the hope in Pastor Joe's eyes.

There was the weekend when Avery, Isabelle, Celia, and I worked with a youth group. I got to wrangle a dozen junior high boys, run them around a ranch house for hours with cardboard tubes for swords and shaving cream for epic battles of masculine feat. At the end of it, they gave me a stone square with a passage from Proverbs engraved on the front, their signatures on the back. It still hangs on my wall. One of the boys asked Jesus into his heart that weekend.

I share this as a means of saying that it was not a waste.

It never is.

I didn't see it at the time.

I think I am only starting to see it now.

I date Celia, Isabelle's best friend, for a week and a half, if you can call that dating.

We get together because we know we are losing Avery and Isabelle.

We break up for the same reason.

There are now only thirteen or so people, Avery and me included, who come to The Well.

It's been falling apart for some time. My preaching is mediocre. We keep singing the same songs.

One evening we try to have Communion.

I have the email, still, even though I have deleted so many of them, in which Avery tells me he will be unable to come to a party for me because he will be with Isabelle, but he will make sure to show up the Saturday we plan on having Communion.

I will make sure to show up.

I read that line over and over, trying to make sense of it.

I try to understand.

I try to piece together exactly what he believed he was doing, saying he was a minister to these people, but he would have to fit them into his schedule. I try to align this with the other things that happened, with the other times he couldn't be bothered to meet to plan the service or the times he ignored my phone calls—I learned it from Aaron Sorkin: four rings to voice mail, they aren't there; two rings to voice mail, they're ignoring you.[20]

But then I have to confront myself.

What was I doing?

I have to address the part of me that, in the on-campus restaurant Saturday morning the day I was to preach, I haphazardly wove verses together hoping something that sounded true would come out. I have to confront the point at which I stopped caring, at which it became a job to do and not a ministry to serve.

Thirteen of us stand outside the parking lot of the church in a field, for reasons I believe are to be symbolic, and we pass around a French loaf from the grocery store and a cup of grape juice. On my instruction, we tear a piece for each other, pass it around, then dip our bread in the cup.

"Are we done?"

Avery, holding Isabelle, right after the last person has dipped. "Yes," I hear myself say. "We're done."

It was around this time that Sarah-Jane and I began to collaborate on an academic article for a journal on Marie de France studies, about one of those tales in that book SJ had handed me as being a reinterpretation of the David and Bathsheba story from the Old Testament. For most of the summer, I was buried in the library, trying to learn Old French and medieval Latin, looking up past projects and hunting down articles. While SJ was in Paris on research leave, she would send me emails in Waco telling me what I needed to accomplish that day, and I had about six hours to get twelve hours of work done. I pulled a half-dozen all-nighters and fell in and out of love with the Middle Ages every other day.

Somewhere between the frenzy of discovery and the patient work of searching I became a scholar. Being a scholar meant I could ask big questions and then go searching for the answers. That's all I had ever really wanted to do.

I spend the last portion of the summer house-sitting for a friend in Waco with Avery. We spend ridiculous amounts of time watching TV and hiking, nearly burning down the kitchen a half dozen times and being idiots because we could be. We light a few things on fire and attempt to rocket launch a few others. We talk about The Well a little here and there, but more and more we let those conversations trail off into nothingness. They are there and not there, we know we are supposed to be doing something for God, but we don't press the question.

Sometimes a message from Addison pops up on my computer, checking in, and in a flurry of words we talk more and more until neither of us can ignore that something has changed, which we promptly dismiss as being foolish, impossible, unfair to Avery.

Avery spends a lot of time with Isabelle, who made arrangements to be in Waco for the summer too. She comes over often, and I try to do things to integrate her more into our lives. I ask her around for dinner, I ask her what sorts of food she likes, and I spend a half day carefully planning a meal to try and impress her, to show her that I thought she belonged.

I didn't catch it.

I didn't catch that I was the one being invited to integrate with *them*. I didn't catch that I was being invited over to their place, not to ours. I didn't catch that Avery and I didn't talk about church anymore, that what we talked about was a future of *what ifs* in which he and Isabelle were already together.

It was so plain. It was so obvious.

But I just kept getting up from the table asking if I could get anyone anything because I didn't have to think about it if I kept busy with my hands.

"You know man, I'd be okay if you and Addison ever wanted to date."

Avery said that to me once, after I had cooked him dinner and we were watching something on TV.

"What do you mean?" I asked him, carefully.

He gave me a knowing look.

"You guys should go for it, see what happens," he shrugged.

I called her that night.

"I'd like that."

She said it with a kind of distance.

"I'm coming back to Baylor for the fall term. You and me. How about that? I had always kind of—"

"Don't say always."

"You're right."

We talked a bit more. I went to bed happy that night. At least, I thought that was what happiness had felt like before.

Avery and I go to the park the day before I am to head home for a few weeks before returning to campus for the start of fall term. We've worked out just before, grabbed quick showers, and had taken his car up to the top of the highest hill, sitting out over the water when he passes me a cigar. I have only ever smoked once before this, but I ease back into the rhythm and fill my mouth with the taste of death.

We talk about The Well, about our meetings with Joe, and how Avery is increasingly dissatisfied with the whole thing, how it is falling apart, how he doesn't feel God in it anymore. I have known this was coming. I have been keeping a quiet tally in my head of all the times we spent talking more about Isabelle than God. I have begun to wonder more about the signs I have kept ignoring, but I hold this half-revelation close, take in another mouth of smoke, press into the world the darkness of my breath.

How did we start talking about Isabelle? It's happened again, slipped so quickly from something else to her. I start thinking about Joan Didion's *Year of Magical Thinking*, about how every little thing becomes a touchstone of return, how language itself folds in and captures us, tinges everything we will ever say with a memory that haunts its meaning.

Avery says something. Something else. He says a few more things. He admits something.

I open my mouth and then close it. I forget the cigar in my hand and light a dead piece of grass on fire, which I quickly put out by spitting on it.

He is looking at me carefully. He is handing me something he has yet to tell anyone else. I can tell because of the fracturing in his gaze, the same way he used to tell me things about his parents, about all the tiny fears.

The words are always haunted with meaning now.

And then I understand. I understand so completely that I stop seeing for a moment.

It's over. We're over. The Well is over.

We stop talking then, altogether. We go see a movie, and then I go to bed. I wake up two hours later and get in my car and drive home in the middle of the night.

I don't call him for those two weeks I am away. There is nothing left to say.

Five

DESERT

I MOVE BACK TO BAYLOR early, before classes begin, in late August 2009.

I'm beginning the term as a student trustee in the Honors Residential College, a position that largely consists of talking appreciatively of the college to any donor willing to listen. It's easy work in that regard, when you love the institution, when you see the good of it, feel the good of it, there's a natural tendency to want others to share in the vision. The College has fostered in me a sense of wonder, of needing rootedness in the words gone before, and I find myself increasingly hungry for the fixedness of those gone before me while everything else solid in my life seemed to be melting into air.[21]

I'm moving boxes of books, moving the ancients, into our dorm room, the room I shall share with Avery, when he and Isabelle walk up.

"Hey, man," he says casually.

"Hey."

Isabelle asks me carefully, "How are you?"

We three stand in the unspoken for a moment, so full it could burst us, until I deflate: "I'm good."

95

Was I making a point?

Was I purposefully using the idiomatic *I'm good* instead of the grammatically correct *I'm well*?

Was I doing it so they would hear it, hear my defiance of them? I think probably not, but I wouldn't be above doing it.

Addison and I sit on a bench somewhere on campus at dusk, late August. The heat sits with us, around us, and one of us makes an offhand comment about how it makes fools of us all.

"He doesn't want to do it anymore. He told me he doesn't care about The Well, Pastor Joe, any of it. He says he just needs time to be."

Addison looks at me then, studies me. She puts one hand over mine and whispers so carefully, as if her words would break me, "Maybe that's for the best. Maybe it's time for you to step back too."

Thirteen people at Communion.

Are we done?

Yes.

I oscillate between anger and relief, middle between them, and nod.

"We are not now what we thought we would be then."

I turn and look at her, the way she looks at me, soft and comforting, reassuring me that she sees me for who I want to be as much as for who I am.

"But what about all the people?" I ask it halfheartedly, because she is looking at me with seriousness, with the question that I can't ask myself aloud, even if I have asked it every day since thirteen people at Communion: what people?

I call Pastor Joe and tell him The Well is going to go on hold for now, but that I will see him in church on Sunday. He says he understands. I resist replying that I don't. I send out a Facebook message to everyone letting them know we are on hiatus for the time being. I still have the message. I hadn't read it in years:

What a journey it's been. At some point, though, we all must come to a place where we realize that we may have in our haste and zeal and want to see the Lord move we end up doing our own thing and claiming God's movement when in reality it's just our influence and deeds. That explains this latter bit. What came before, that was God and His movement. We don't know what it meant, we don't know what it means, we don't know what it will mean, but we know that God moved and has now moved us somewhere different.

I close the message with something else. Something simple.

We don't know what it will mean.

I still carry that as a question in me, even now.

I carry it differently, but it lingers. It curls up with me—like that heat in August—in bed in the darkness and wraps its arms around my neck. Some nights I reject it. Some nights I let it stay. I've never been sure what reaction would be the most faithful. I've never been sure what reaction would be the most true.

Addison and I broke up.

She confessed to me under a magnolia tree one night that while we had been chatting over the summer she had been in an on-and-off relationship with another guy. It wasn't that part that gutted me, the part about the other guy. The blow that struck hard was how I found out, casually, by accident, because I made a passing comment about something that hit enough of a nerve that she felt guilty, opened her mouth just enough, and let it all come tumbling out.

I realized she never would have told me otherwise. More, I realized this was the way with her. I began to put together in my mind all the times she would do something foolish, unsafe—there was the ride she gave to the homeless man who approached her, the walking home down that one street alone in the middle of the night—and a month later I would find out, by chance, and there was nowhere to put the anger, displaced and wandering, so it only circled back in on me.

There was no fight, just a statement of terms. We were and then we were not.

I don't remember who walked away from that tree first.

On my birthday, The Family put together a simple celebration, dinner and a movie.

Addison took a poster board and drew a bust of Virgil on it, scribed Latin across the top, and had everyone sign. Meredith wrote a simple, *Hope you have a great year!* and Avery, *Happy Birthday, man!* They had invited a few other people, new people, new friends, who wrote messages too that were that absurd mix of too friendly and too distant all at once.

The meal was hollow. We were playacting, trying to pretend like things were as they always had been, even though we all knew how very broken it all was. No one mentioned The Well. No one really mentioned me. I was put at the head of the table while everyone else chatted amongst themselves. Addison would look over from time to time, but I was still mad, mad enough. I was so alone in the midst of so much, but then again we all were.

A crowd of lonely people can only ever hope for the taste of ash.

There's a picture, somewhere, of that dinner. Avery and I beside each other. I look so unhappy. It unsettles me now. I look into eyes that seem dead. I don't see myself. Or I refuse to.

Isabelle was there. It was the overtness that always jarred me.

When The Family went on to the movies, about to buy tickets, Avery looked over and noticed I was a bit despondent. I had played the evening so well until that moment, when I thought no one was looking, and I let the sadness register.

"You all right?"

Why did it always sound these days like an accusation? (An interjection: what had happened that my friends, if they were that then, could no longer see how dead my eyes had become?)

"I think I just want to go back. I'm not feeling well."

They drove me back. Isabelle and Avery. They drove me until Isabelle said she wanted frozen yogurt and we stopped, and I had to wait for her to put sprinkles on her chocolate swirl before finally making it back to campus. I shrugged off Avery's offer of an Advil, walked into our dorm room, turned off the lights, and got into bed.

It wasn't that my birthday had been dinner and a movie. It wasn't that I had a poster board of a dead Latin poet I had once mused I would do my thesis on but had since given up. It wasn't that all the well-wishing had been so empty. It was that the dinner and the movie felt from planning to execution like obligation. I would have been so very happy with dinner and a movie if what accompanied it was being seen, being loved, being wanted.

It was done because it's the thing you do. We lived our lives together, in those days, based out of obligation.

I suppose that was the night something broke. That was the last time The Family was ever all together.

We weren't family anymore.

Dr. Harmon—Constance—emails me that we should get coffee and catch up. We meet at Common Grounds, and over my cappuccino and her jasmine tea with nine packets of sugar stirred in, we discuss the Middle Ages. Constance is a medievalist, particularly interested in Italy and Saint Francis and Saint Clare.

The word *saint* drops between us like a bowling ball. I see it and yet can't quite touch it, accept its presence but recoil at its possibility. It is too Catholic, too mystical, and if I had feared before that Constance was not a Christian, I now fear she is a zealot.

She studies me carefully while I talk about the research I did for the article with SJ, about my interest in stories and the fabric of memory. She lets me talk, so I keep talking. I talk for an hour. At some point when I am still she looks at me for a long moment, looks at me hard, direct: "You have no center right now."

It is matter of fact.

"I don't."

She sits back and takes her lower lip into her mouth, chews it, then says: "Francis has a prayer — " she stops — "no, not yet. You're not ready for that. Francis has a way of seeing the world: he calls the moon sister and the sun brother. Do you understand?"

I drain my cappuccino.

"Yes."

I say this because I'm proud. She keeps looking at me.

"No."

I say this because I am curious.

"Think of it like this: in the Middle Ages, gravity was explained by saying that angels, the handmaids of God, were dragging falling objects down to the earth. Today, we call it science, we call it gravity, we say that objects on Earth theoretically fall at negative nine-point-eight meters per second squared, but is it possible while that is fact, so are the angels in a way? Is it possible that both coexist, that the negative nine-point-eight is angelic, that while the angels might not be fact, they are nonetheless true?"

I stare at her. I think she's a heretic. I think she might be right.

I think she has something that I want to have, but I don't know how to ask for it.

"You should pray wilder."

This she says while rising.

"Good to see you. We should do this again sometime."

And she leaves. I stare into the emptiness of my cappuccino cup so that I don't have to stare into the emptiness of me.

A week later, a book arrives in my campus mailbox. It is an anthology of the writings of Saint Francis and Saint Clare. There is a note, hastily scratched onto a Post-it on the cover: *For the journey.*

Avery and I don't speak anymore.

We inhabit the same living space, but we don't acknowledge the other.

Once, I fold a pile of his laundry in an attempt at some sort of kindness. I am still trying to piece something together. I am still trying to make sense of the shards. When he walks in to find the laundry folded, I on my bed reading a book. I hear him push air out of his lungs with a kind of practiced defiance. I am pathetic. This is what he wants me to hear.

I hear it. It sits on the bed beside me while I read. I don't look it in the eye.

The next morning I call my father and tell him it's over. I sit on a bench on campus during parents' weekend, pools of freshman parents wandering around loudly and excitedly, the prospect of beginnings, and I call my parent to say it's all fallen apart. The Well. Avery. Addison. It's over. It's so over.

"What are you going to do now?"

"I guess what I have to do."

"What's that?"

"I don't know anymore."

⋈

Addison and I get back together in October.

We meet for lunch to chat as friends, and by the end we're holding hands. She smiles at me, I at her, and we silently make some sort of treaty of togetherness. We are polite in this. We are polite about the lie. The lie of us. This is the unspoken bit, the part that we ignore: we don't love each other. We are good friends, but we are not in love. But we are so alone. We might as well be alone together.

As part of my Great Texts major, I took a class with Ralph Wood in Christian spirituality. The course is variable, ever-changing; the reading list a smattering of people's writings throughout the history of the Faith selected at the discretion of the instructor. For our term, Dr. Wood chose the *Four Centuries on Love* from Maximus the Confessor, the prayers of Saint Catherine of Siena, *Grace Abounding* by John Bunyan, Bonhoeffer's *Life Together*, hymns from John Wesley and Isaac Watts, Negro spirituals, and Gregory of Nyssa's *The Life of Moses*, which we ended up never reading or using.

Dr. Wood is a self-described Bapto-Catholic, fixed in a community of free prayer and river baptisms, grafted into the larger family of faith, to the Tradition. Tradition is important to him. He stood in class and stared us down, our presumptions about God, about how sure we were about the One so very other and yet so very near. He stressed our need for fluency, our need to be able to navigate the larger conversation about what it meant to confess Christ as Lord regardless of the denomination in which we made our home. "All of them have their ills," he said simply, gazing around the room, "but if they, as the Scripture tells us, are keeping with the teaching of the apostles, they have something to teach us."

Dr. Wood was a great apologist for the diversity of God. Lean too far toward pure, unmoored cultural evangelicalism, and he would sharply interject a reminder that the Church was older than youth groups in the mid-nineties; praise the old ways and days gone by as the highlight of true Christian expression, hc would quickly point to the outbreaking of the Spirit in contemporary Third World countries. What he wanted most from us was to love God broadly, to want the whole of the Church to be our conversation partners, not just our little enclave of belief we had tacitly agreed upon in our outposts of conservative safety in the Bible Belt.

He chose Maximus because the Confessor said God had created the cosmos to ever process forth from God, was always in harmony with God; Catherine because she yearned to carry Jesus within her how Mary once had; Bunyan because we make too light of sin and too much of showing off our confession; Bonhoeffer for the harmony of Christian unity; Wesley for the hunger to be like God, Watts for the desperation for God to be known as incarnate man; the spirituals to teach that the children of Israel are still in exodus from Egypt, and Nyssa, forgotten, but needed for a reason I would not understand until years later.

> *His dying crimson, like a robe,*
> *Spreads o'er His body on the tree;*
> *Then I am dead to all the globe,*
> *And all the globe is dead to me.*
> (From "When I Survey the Wondrous Cross," a hymn of Watts)

"Can anyone tell me why we don't sing this verse in Baptist churches?" He looked around the room.

"Hands!"

This was his usual command, we were all supposed to know

the answer, so all our hands were supposed to spring up at once. No one raised their hand. We were lost.

After a moment, he explained, "It sounds too Catholic. In Communion, in the Eucharist, we say that the death of Christ and the promise of his resurrection are made known to us in a unique and terrible way: his dying crimson, his blood, covers his own body such that I become dead to this world, the world to me, and I become like Christ, unified with God uniquely and particularly. If you are in a nonliturgical tradition, however, you tend to believe that Communion is simply a memory of what Jesus did on the Cross. At best it demands something of you, but most of the time we brush over it entirely. We say we are thinking about him, but we fail to ask him to actually reside within us."

Out of the corner of my eye, I made note, not for the first time, of the athletic guy named Jerry, who would come to class in running shorts after going for fourteen miles on a light workout day and had been labeled by Dr. Wood the token Calvinist of our semester. I could see Jerry taking notes, along with rather direct commentary on just what he thought of all of Dr. Wood's theology. It was without tact, but it was funny.

I knew two things immediately: Jerry was an ass and I wanted to be his friend.

I started spending a lot of time at Common Grounds.

The shabby house-turned-coffee shop became my home. I couldn't hang around my dorm room under threat of running into Avery and Isabelle, and I felt displaced in the community life of the College, somehow a part of it but not. I would take up a corner of Common Grounds, pull out a reading assignment or my Bible or that copy of the words of Francis and Clare, read and write and drink dry cappuccino after dry cappuccino, while I made conversation with the empty air about all the questions of self that were beginning to bubble up within me.

Did I really hear?

Was this asked of God or asked of myself?

I still don't know.

Sometimes Addison came along, flipping through notes and drumming her pen against her teacup. She would stare at me but wouldn't quite connect, would keep going, all the way through me. She wanted so badly to understand. I wanted so badly to tell her that she didn't need to.

Contemplation is a gaze of faith, fixed on Jesus.[22]

I would turn that line from Saint Clare's second letter to Saint Agnes over and over while I waited to order my coffee, thinking about whether or not I had heard God, we had heard God, if Avery still wanted to hear God, and if maybe this was the season of trying simply to see God, not to listen for signs but to look for them, to think on Jesus and therefore think on the world as completely his. A cosmic joke, I supposed, in which the punch line was how ridiculously abundant God could be.

Then doubt would circle back around, and I would be back to questioning my worth, the hearing, the foundations of the world.

The foundations of the world.

There was a stone statue by the register, next to the tip jar, a man with a shaved head holding a little bird.

"What's that?" I asked once.

A barista turned, half-shrugged.

"That's Saint Francis. He's been here for years."

I have my first conversation with Grant in the lobby of our dormitory in the late evening.

Grant is impossibly good. There are times when I can't look

at him too directly: the goodness of him overwhelms the parts of me that want to stay unchanged by that good. He is tall, rooted, and the first time I saw him, I mentioned to the person I was with that he could have walked right out of a film set in the Regency era in which he would have been a priest. When I think of Grant, I think of evening prayer and careful homilies. He is pastoral but convicted. I learned gentleness from him, but I learned steady passion too.

We are both in Dr. Wood's class, discussing something about the assigned reading for a few minutes and somehow meander into baptism. The when, the how, the why. We disagree, firmly, but casually. We laugh. We push. We ask questions that expect more from each other than lines rehearsed from spoken and unspoken catechisms. We make plans to work together on a project for class; we make plans for coffee.

As I walk up the stairs that night, a few hours later, as the latch to the door of my room turns and clicks, I realize that I have been heard. I have spent a few hours speaking to someone who actually heard me. I am awed.

It was near the beginning of October on a Sunday morning, as I was driving around downtown Waco, that I told God that I couldn't pray anymore. I'm not quite sure how I ended up in the parking lot of St. Paul's Episcopal Church, if I simply turned a corner and was there at the place where Sixth and Columbus Avenue intersect; if I simply saw the word *Episcopal* and decided it was other enough than *Baptist* that it just might work. Regardless, I ended up in the parking lot, watching people walk inside, telling God that I was done, that I was empty, that I no longer had the words to form prayer.

God told me to go inside.

(God told me. I pause on those words as I write them. I observe them there and question them. I fear questioning them too much, even now.)

When I walked in, toward the sanctuary, there wasn't anyone there. I could see that inside was burgundy carpet, a high altar in the back, ribs like an overturned ship forming the roof, stained glass of saints and of Jesus, and candles all along the front, unlit.

"Were you looking for something?"

I turned around to find an older woman, holding a stack of programs.

"Is there a service today?"

"Oh yes!" She beamed, laughing a bit and waving me forward, "Just down in the parish hall for today." She gestured its direction and then called over her shoulder, "The peace of the Lord!"

I didn't say anything back. I followed the corridor down to the parish hall, pushed open a door, and found myself in a tangle of folding chairs, barking dogs, a turtle, a gaggle of children clinging to families, and an altar at the front of what appeared to serve normally as a combination gym and cafeteria. I was handed a program, what I would learn to call "Holy Communion: Rite II" someday, and slipped my way into the back onto a folding chair.

Everyone stood when the cross entered, slowed, before the choir and the priests, up unto the altar. They bowed as it passed. A dog barked. We sang something about the whole creation belonging to God, about how it was all completely and utterly God's. When the hymn finished, a woman, in the white robe of a priest with a stole about her that depicted the animals walking into Noah's ark, pronounced: "Blessed be God, Father, Son, and Holy Spirit."

As she did so, everyone crossed themselves. I crossed myself too. A step behind. But I did.

"And blessed be his kingdom, now and forever, amen." The congregation replied.

I looked at my program, found the words printed there, bolded for me to say, prayers written down for me when I didn't have the words. I wondered at it, felt the ripple of it, the power they held, and felt God tell me to calm my heart.

"Today," the priest continued, "we are a messy bunch. On this day, we bless the animals God has entrusted to our care and commend them back to him and his service, as we celebrate the Feast of Saint Francis, who loved God's creation so dearly."

I stood completely still, disbelieving. The Feast of Saint Francis.

I marveled for the next hour: how the Scripture was read, how the homily was simple, how people passed the peace of God to one another so fluidly that you thought it was a thing that was in fact given, that had weight when you put it into someone's hand. When it was time for Communion, I walked forward, I knelt, and I crossed my arms over my chest. The program had said that I would receive a blessing instead of the Body and Blood if I was uncomfortable with receiving.

I was uncomfortable. I was unable to accept the crimson robe, the dead globe, and my own death with it.

"What is your name?"

The priest lifted my face to meet her eyes.

"Preston."

"Preston," she repeated, "I am Mother Andrea, and I bless you in the name of the Father, the Son, and the Holy Spirit," and as she said it, she made the sign of the cross on my forehead.

"May God defend your heart, strengthen your spirit, and bring you into the life everlasting. Amen."

"Amen," I repeated.

After the service, when I walked out into the courtyard of the church, a small bird took flight, like the bird in the palm of the statue Francis, a stone bird given wings and the impossible lightness to fly. I thought maybe something like that was happening to me. I kept thinking it for the next handful of months, every Sunday morning that I attended St. Paul's, every Sunday that I got close to receiving Communion, then not.

"You're not ready for that." Constance had said.

Not yet.

In desperation for community, I asked Jerry, Grant, and Evan, my floor's RA, if we could meet together for a Bible study at Common Grounds. Evan is one of the most tenderhearted people I have ever known. The first time we had a true conversation was walking campus for hours as I explained slowly and guardedly the tensions between Avery and me, and it was Evan who told me that Avery would be studying abroad the following semester and I would no longer have to live with him.

"He said things hadn't worked out."

I blinked several times. Avery had robbed me of even this, making the first move out of the misery of it all.

"They hadn't."

The four of us would gather at Common Grounds and slowly work through a book of the Bible, each taking turns leading. We read Galatians first, which consisted of me fighting with Jerry about Calvinism, and Grant and Evan working carefully toward peace.

What I remember is half, if not fully, fact, but I remember the time we fed a homeless man who walked up to us and asked for food and the time we prayed for each other in the old ways of praying, slow and confident with the gentle brush of reverence. It saved my life, I think. It was the place where I met Jesus outside of St. Paul's, when I couldn't see him anywhere else: in the face of Evan, the face of Grant, the face of Jerry. I met Jesus again.

I suppose remembering fact doesn't matter in the same way in light of that sort of truth.

⋊⋉

The last time I saw Avery, we got an early lunch at a dump of a Mexican restaurant somewhere near the highway in Waco. It was a Sunday. I had just come from St. Paul's. We talked about nothing, nothing I can remember, except this:

"You're going to the Episcopal church?"

"Yeah."

He sneered at me. Sneered. I had never seen that expression on his face before.

"You really like all that stand up, sit down, cross yourself?"

I stared at him for a long time. I think for a moment I looked hurt, but a moment later I looked resolute.

"I do."

I didn't even bother to challenge him. I got up, paid for his meal, and left.

I sat in my car in the parking lot, threw my hand against the steering wheel, hard, and shouted, "Damn it!"

And in the stillness that followed, I pursed my lips.

"Don't damn it."

I prayed it hard and loud but I never opened my mouth.

"Please don't damn it. Please don't. Please don't. Please don't."

I prayed it the entire day.

After a while, I stop going to the church where The Well started and failed.

It wasn't a single decision, but a series of small ones.

It was just too sad. Or I was.

Early November. Phyllis Tickle stands at the front of the lecture hall of my dorm, talking about the changing nature of the church.

She says we seem to cycle historically every five hundred years, get restless, need the change and the shift and the splintering to keep fresh in the Spirit. She is using the emerging church as her example, but she mentions that young evangelicals may be drawn increasingly to liturgical practice as well.

"They will crave the words of life being handed to them, instead of always having to produce them for themselves."

After googling her, I found that she had put together a four-volume series of daily prayer for the year. I bought all of them. When they arrived, I pulled the copy for autumn, which I came to learn was called Ordinary Time, and began to pray.

The stone heart, winged by these words from someone else. I began to feel the lift. Just a whisper at first.

Between Dr. Wood and the prayer books, I began to learn about the Church Year.

Liturgical denominations do not mark time by months and days but by seasons, feasts, and fasts. It is how there is a feast day for Saint Francis in early October and why the colors on the altar or in the church as a whole change from time to time.

The cycle begins in Advent, in preparation for the coming of Christ, four weeks before the Sunday of the week of Christmas. Then Christmas is twelve days, followed by Epiphany, the season in which we reflect on the slow revealing of Jesus as the Messiah in the Gospels. Then comes Lent for forty days, not counting Sundays, when we mark with fasting a different sort of preparation, the preparation for a different coming of Christ, in a way, then Holy Week, the great cataclysmic series of Maundy Thursday, Good Friday, Holy Saturday, and Easter. Then Easter lasts for fifty days, ten more than Lent, the days of feasting and glory and wonder at the awe of God. Afterward, a blur. The Ascension, then

Pentecost, and then the longest season, which follows Pentecost, called Ordinary Time.

Ordinary Time is a curious season. It can feel tedious quickly. Nothing is exactly happening. No one is excited about buying presents for family and no one is musing about what they are fasting from for Lent. No one is really doing much of anything except being, hanging around. There's not quite the excited joy of Easter and no frenzy of fire that is Pentecost.

But that is the point, I think, the reason that the color of Ordinary Time is green. It is the season that is also called, at times, Kingdom Time. The season in which the church flourishes and grows. I suppose it's supposed to be the season of the work, of the devotion to whatever God intends. Sometimes aching, sometimes boring.

Sometimes there is growth, but you won't see it until much later, sometime around Advent, sometime in Easter, sometime, someday, maybe.

Ordinary Time is maybe time.

Maybe God will come back.

August. Years later. I have *The Divine Hours* open, the prayers for summer. I work slowly through the morning passage, mark the hours with the words of life. I've been doing this now for nearly half a decade, in cycles and seasons, using Phyllis's woven passages of prayer and lament and praise.

The image of weaving. I return to it often in the season I was unwoven.

Phyllis was one of the means by which God rewove me. She still is. Every day, I am unwoven and rewoven. The words get into my bones.

Sometimes I forget them.

But sometimes I remember. I remember more now than I used to, which I suppose is what some would call progress. Some sanctification.

Maybe.

"Where are you?"

SJ calls me when I'm at the turn on the highway that points me home. I'm an hour from campus. I inform her of this. It's Thanksgiving break. I'm skipping my last class. Not hers—Dr. Wood's. I'm skipping to go home because it doesn't really matter if I make class or not. Nothing feels much like it matters anymore.

"I can't do it." I am clipped in response.

She already knows what I can't do. She knows that I have been Avery's roommate for the past four months, how after the announcement in the park, everything else broke too. She doesn't know the details, but she can feel the possibilities. We spoke of it once, briefly, because she could tell something had happened, and she stopped me before I said too much.

"Come back. Go to class."

She was insistent. I said nothing.

"Preston. You have to come back," she pushed. "You have to come back, because there will come a point in your life when it won't be packing your car and leaving campus. I know more about this than you understand. One day, you'll be looking up flights to Paris, packing bags, and running from your life. You have to stop fleeing to Paris, Preston. You have to stop."

I pull over. It is gray out, sun streaking over the fields bent low with the briskness of the air. I sit in silence for a few minutes. I address God beside me.

"This is your doing."

God says nothing.

I turn my car around and head back. I drive in silence the whole way, turning over the past four months, then further back to when we first met, Avery and I staying up late and talking about a future that would never and could never be. I feel like an idiot. I feel like I have been played. I feel like I am just as guilty and that I don't know how to ask forgiveness anymore.

SJ meets me on the steps of the girls' dormitory, armed with a Chanel bag and plastic silverware. She hands me a heated up frozen Moroccan TV dinner and a banana.

"Go," she says simply, then turns and walks away.

It was, in its ordinariness, one of the most formative moments of my life.

On the first Sunday of Advent, near the end of November, I was in the third row from the back and to the left at St. Paul's.

"In Advent, we prepare our hearts for the coming of Jesus just as Mary prepared herself to be his mother. We take on in spirit what she did physically, so that we, like her, may bear the Christ within us."

It is that last bit that arrests me, the bearing Christ within. I reach out beside me to feel the empty space that I imagined God occupied, and during the Prayers of the People I say nothing, pray nothing, except that I want to bear Christ within me.

In Dr. Wood's class, we've just finished the prayers of Saint Catherine of Siena. *O Mary, bearer of fire.* I want to bear that fire within me. I want to know it once more. I want to be awed by him. I don't need the tempestuous passion of loud faith, but I need faith. I am hungry for it. Hungry to be bested by God.

"Show me."

It was rasped and quiet, perhaps not even spoken aloud.

During the Confession, I can feel every fiber within me tense, I can feel my heart fall and lift on the turn of the paragraph prayer.

Things done and undone.

I have been undone. These past months, I have been unwoven.

When Father Chuck makes the sign of the cross over us, says we are forgiven, I find myself making it too, making it over myself, embodied prayer against the disquiet of my spirit, and it is as if the Jesus of the stained glass above the altar, the Shepherd Jesus, looks at me and says, "You are forgiven, Preston. Go. Sin no more."

When I stood, I didn't quite make sense of what I was expecting to do. I walked down the aisle, beside the baptismal fount and up to the altar, even up to the altar of God. (There is a point to the walk in high churches: we begin in Baptism and abide by the Eucharist, we begin in our confession that Christ is Lord and abide by our proclamation that the Lord is Christ.)

I knelt down at the altar rail, made the sign of the cross, and after stealing a look at the person beside me, cupped my hands into the shape of receiving, right hand over left. Mother Andrea, white robe dipping against the burgundy carpet, placed a broken shard of blessed bread into my hands, touched the crown of my head, made the sign of the cross, and said, "Preston, this is the Body of Christ, broken for you. Take this, remembering Christ died for you, and feed on him in your heart by faith with thanksgiving." The cup followed. I dipped my shard into it at the words, "The Blood of Christ, the cup of salvation."

Then I consumed the drenched shard, felt sweetness and fire, felt a burn prick and soothe my heart. I felt the shard pierce me — the sword that would pierce Mary's heart, maybe that was the point — and yet cauterize me. It undid me. It made me whole. In a second, then it was gone.

I crossed myself, rose, and walked back to my seat while the choir began to sing, "I want to walk as a child of the Light, I want to follow Jesus ..."

There is a line from a poem of Elizabeth Barrett Browning:

Earth's crammed with heaven,
And every common bush afire with God.[23]

I sat in the pew, staring up at the altar, completely at peace, completely on fire.

God was not beside me.

I felt, so quietly I couldn't listen too hard for it lest I miss it, that he was within me.

Instead of these things you gave your people food of
angels,
and without their toil you supplied them from heaven
with bread ready to eat,
providing every pleasure and suited to every taste.
For your sustenance manifested your sweetness toward
your children;
and the bread, ministering to the desire of the one who
took it,
was changed to suit everyone's liking.[24]

I read this in the Wisdom of Solomon years later. It's about the manna God gave the children of Israel in the desert. Except it's not. It's about manna, but it's also about the Eucharist. It is about Body and Blood. It's about bread from heaven. It's about *give us this day our daily bread*.

I couldn't know that when I first went up to that altar in St. Paul's—even up unto to the altar of God, as the Scottish Episcopal liturgy words it—I wasn't ready for it. I couldn't bear to know it. *Changed to suit everyone's liking.* Maximus the Confessor said that each person is given in the Eucharist the grace they need to do the work God has given them to accomplish, however seemingly large or small. It's something about Jesus, how Jesus is infinite and yet finite, how he is very God and yet very Man. This is, somehow, contained and yet not contained in the bread and wine.

I can hold that meaning, the fullness of it, now. Except I can't. It's too much. Body and Blood. Him. It's too much. I suppose that means I get it: because I don't. But to want to know it is to want to know him. *I shall go up unto the altar, even up unto the altar of God.*

I think it's a way of asking Jesus into your heart.

My parents abided in a strange place of adjustment when it came to my attendance at St. Paul's, which I readily admitted I was also confused by. I didn't feel that I would join the church formally, let alone be confirmed Episcopalian, but it was the only place I was going that I truly felt the peace of God at the time.

Being still financially dependent on my parents, however, I was not quite beyond their authority. They weren't comfortable releasing me, not just yet, from the tradition of faith I had been raised in and made the request that if I was going to keep going to St. Paul's that I attend a Baptist church as well. This is what resulted in my two church Sundays, a tradition I would keep until my senior year. During this season, I would rise early and go by myself to St. Paul's for the first service, then go meet Addison for coffee before the two of us went on to some nondescript Baptist church, bouncing around them looking for a place to land.

In retrospect, my parents were gracious in this. They could have very well forbidden me from going to St. Paul's, a move that would be surprising but was not beyond them. Rather, they encouraged questioning. They asked me to consider exactly what I was doing and why. The problem was I wanted immediate acceptance; I still wanted them to agree completely with every choice I made, so I pushed them harshly when they didn't.

"What do you believe about infant baptism?" my father asks me once, sharply, but only because I have goaded him the entire time, have pressed hard into his sensitivities because I want so desperately to be other than the experience that had wounded me.

"I don't know."

And I was telling the truth.

"I still think it's wrong."

And I did. For the most part. I was questioning it, but I also didn't much care about it. I didn't really care that the theology was different, only that it was different.

Notice the motivation: to be other than. For all the beauty that brought me into St. Paul's, for all the significance of finding myself there, I was motivated in part by my desire to flee. I let the failure of The Well be the failure of the faith tradition itself. It happened quietly and subtlety, but it made me antagonistic, fretful, mean. It made me resent where I had come from, which is a sort of violence that's hard to take back.

I would argue the points of theology for sport. I made the circle of my thoughts intellectual exercise. I made the circle of my thoughts encompass everything about God, without God.

The beginning of human pride is to forsake the Lord;
the heart has withdrawn from its Maker.[25]

It's sometime late Advent, chilled but not cold. I'm dog-sitting for a friend, bleary-eyed on an early Sunday morning, getting dressed for St. Paul's. I let the dog out the front, his usual routine, but when I come back five minutes later, he's gone.

He does this sometimes, wanders off to a neighbor. It's a street of students, and he loves the attention, especially the older he gets. I feel rushed and angry. I quickly button my shirt and pull on a pair of TOMS before sprinting out the door, calling his name.

"Why do I do this, God?" I had been attempting to pray again. Praying angry was about the best I could manage. "Why do I go to two churches? Why do I care about these questions? Do you even hear me? Do you—"

I find the dog padding up to a blond guy my age putting his bike through a rack, and I feel my stomach sink.

I don't want this, a forced interaction, probably with a guy who is in a frat or super athletic or one of those Baylor golden children who is in a frat, super athletic, *and* ridiculously intelligent—defining myself, still, by the things that I think I am not.

"Is this your dog?" he calls over to me.

I have been seen.

"My friend's," I answer brusquely. "What did you find?" I ask the dog, who looks back at me pointedly. I stare back. I call him over. He doesn't move. I don't really make eye contact with the blond guy while I half-walk, half-drag the dog away.

I'm cursing the dog under my breath, ignoring that something in me has been unsettled.

I had been seen.

The blond guy had actually seen me, I could feel it, right into the pit of the crack of self I had been sitting in, and the reason I kept avoiding his gaze was a simple one, but a terrifying one: his look was impossibly kind.

Notice: a shift so small.

I begin to mark time by the Church Year, not by months.

Notice: it is not so very small a shift.

Avery broke up with Isabelle.

For the spring term, he left for Paris.

The cosmic joke.

><

Epiphany. January.

Even though I had sat in on the ancients course SJ had taught for Great Texts the semester before, I still had to take it officially for a grade in order to have it count in the program. I signed up for her morning section, the only time I could fit it into my course load, and on the first day of spring term walked downstairs to the classroom in my dorm in sweatpants, holding a dry cappuccino from Common Grounds and a falling-apart copy of the *Timaeus* with a pen inside.

I sat in the back row, opening my text and looking over the annotations, trying to keep to myself. SJ entered five minutes late, per first-day tradition, now pleased to find that people had begun to talk amongst themselves about the readings and to form study groups. Word had gotten out. She began to describe Atlantis, a narrative sweep about why it matters that our stories are written down and the importance of committing them to memory.

That had been the charge of Marie de France: we write down these stories, the ancients taught us to, so that generations later people could make sense of the world thanks to what had been handed down. It had been Dr. Wood's insistence, too, that it mattered what Tradition told us about God because faith wasn't in a vacuum. Tradition mattered because if it was just us and the Bible we could get into some real trouble. Tradition wasn't authority in the way people thought of it, a final word that was forever closed, but a vocabulary, a grammar, a slowly learned language that situated the conversation between us and God in the larger scheme of God and time and history and everyone and everything. It was about being handed the story that was ongoing, invited to be within it but encouraged also to know the origins, the roots, the before that our lives were the after of.

St. Paul's was my gesture toward it, toward the faith handed down. The sign of the cross was my gesture toward it. The first time I received the Eucharist was a gesture toward it. These were slow, careful steps into admission that I hadn't known what I was doing with Avery and The Well, that God may or may not have spoken, that it could have very well just been pride. I didn't know, I couldn't know, but I knew I could submit myself, in a way, to the larger language of the Church, to its people, to those gone before.

That kept me afloat. It helped me survive.

I surveyed the room. Fifteen. I knew many of them from around the College. Almost all of them were a class behind me. And then I saw him, the blond guy from December, when the dog had plodded off and found something and was trying to get me to take the point. I looked away.

After class, I was headed out the door when I heard SJ call me back.

"Preston, could you wait a second?"

I turned around to see the blond guy standing with SJ.

"This young man would like to learn about the Great Texts major, and I told him no one was better suited to meet with about it than you. Why don't you guys get a coffee sometime and talk about it?"

"Sure."

I must have sounded hollow, uncertain. He hadn't even opened his mouth and yet the kindness that radiated from him terrified me.

What had I been praying before cursing the dog? *Do you even hear?*

I introduced myself. His name was Samuel. Which means, in the Hebrew, *God heard.*

Six

CONVERSION

SAM AND I MET for coffee at Common Grounds somewhere in early Epiphany 2010.

We talked for hours. We began talking about the Great Texts program but were quickly derailed. Sam was not who I presumed he was. I was not wrong to think him intelligent or athletic, and he did have a brief stint in a fraternity, but I had misunderstood the kindness that processed in front of him. I had confronted it like a challenge, with my emptiness and uncertainty in myself—to face a reflection of what I thought I had been once able to give others unnerved me.

I need to admit, here, the thing I have of yet to speak, but maybe you've picked up on it. What happened with Avery turned me cruel, at least at times. There was a sharpness to my words. Not completely, not to the point that I had become totally hardened, but enough that the edge to me, a desire to cut before I was ever cut again, fought hard against love that was too pure, too self-giving. If I look back on the points of the plot of life up to that particular moment in time, I used to have that kind of love, but I lost it somewhere in the disillusionment.

But Sam is not kind the way most people are kind. He is kind like the world depends on it. Few things grieve him more than harming someone with his words, and he'll drop everything to make it right. That sort of kindness, the kindness that will see the whole of you, felt like a memory. Even trying to write it down is proving a challenge, an almost-not-quite rendition of the events.

It was cold and we were sitting outside, bundled in jackets, drinking hot things in large Styrofoam cups, and because we were two people who cared a lot about the stories of others, we ended up talking for four hours about our lives, our faith, our girlfriends, our hopes and dreams and wonderings.

It was natural. Easy. Yet not. He asked *why* often. It was unsettling. I was so used to *what*.

I told him about Avery. Not everything, not quite. I told him vague things, then a few specific, fighting the want to tell him all of it—and why did I want to? So soon? Sam took it and held it, gave me the room to say just as much of it as I could, even though the saying was unpracticed and I was at times too generous and too flippant, too self-righteous and too self-abasing, but at the end he thanked me.

I was bewildered. Why would he thank me for that? He talked about trust, the trust it takes to share that kind of vulnerability. I blinked at him. Had I been vulnerable? I was numb to it, then. I didn't feel how much I had given, how much I had poured out. I could see it, a bit, in his eyes, that I had given so much without realizing it.

I thought he would leave. It was too much. I was always too much, too extreme, too wrapped up in the hurt. But he only shifted on the bench along the table we occupied, and he stayed. He stayed and told more of his own story, then asked more of mine. We went back and forth like that for another hour, at least, until it was quite late and Sam had to go to the other friends he had already put off once to keep us talking.

Addison called me as he was leaving.

"How'd it go? You've been there for a long time; do you still want to come by?"

"Yes, but I have Bible study with Grant and the rest."

"After?"

It was said with fragility, with tenderness. She wanted to ask for more, but she didn't know how.

"Yes."

After a moment, she pushed, "You sound peaceful."

"I'm not sure what just happened."

There was a pause. A wind picked up over the top of my head, and I could hear the branches of the trees strain.

"Maybe that's for the best."

That semester I took the module for Early Modern Great Texts, which covered, roughly, the literary tradition from about 1500 to 1800. We read Luther, Saint Teresa of Ávila, Hobbes, Descartes, Shakespeare, Milton, and a handful of others. Early Modern structured its engagement with texts around one question posed in Harvard philosopher Charles Taylor's *A Secular Age*: "Why was it virtually impossible not to believe in God in, say, 1500 in our Western society, while in 2000 many of us find this not only easy, but even inescapable?"[26]

From text to text we wandered with the question of disenchantment before us. Where were the clues? Where were the evidences that as we moved into modernity we were losing sight of the holy? We each answered it differently; we each had a suggested methodology of how to approach the *why* of it all. But the common consensus was that knowledge without the temperance of faith was a strange bedfellow. In the Middle Ages, science was considered a handmaiden of God; as you move into modernity, it becomes increasingly God's alleged antagonist.

A correction for this comes by way of Milton's Adam, who

proclaims his desire for understanding to be no more than "the more / To magnify his works, the more we know."[27] And perhaps this too is the reason Saint Teresa is so insistent that "Christ has no body now on earth but yours, no hands but yours, no feet but yours. Yours are the eyes through which to look out Christ's compassion to the world. Yours are the feet with which he is to go about doing good; yours are the hands with which he is to bless men now."[28]

If the end of knowledge is not to magnify God or to be Christ unto one another, then to what avail is it? What we saw in Early Modern was the increasing disconnect between knowledge as the celebration of God's wonder and more the explanation that put God away.

I wonder.

I wonder if that was not, in a sense, what I was doing at St. Paul's. For a time my need to be other than what I had been raised with was an expedition in collecting enough knowledge to explain away The Well, to reinterpret the events of hearing and certainty with enough doubt that I could distance myself from them. I wanted knowledge just so I could box that time of my life and not have to account for it again. I didn't want to consider that there may have been reason and even holy work in the failing of it. So I sat on my hands and crossed my feet and shut my eyes and took in all the information I could to avoid the hard work of being Christ to others.

But I didn't know that, then.

I've only come to realize that now.

I think I'll go to Italy.

I arrange to meet with the coordinator for study abroad and talk *Italia* for twenty minutes while I sip an iced tea and promise I'll study the language and the culture and art and will go to that one place he loves on the corner of that one street and that other street with the blue door.

I call my parents and tell them I think I'll go to Florence for a semester.

"And do what?"

"Anything but this."

I didn't go to Italy.

I still haven't.

My father asks me if I want to go to England to work for a Baptist church for the summer. I know that originally this was an offer he was going to make to Avery and me.

I say yes. Hollowly. Uncertainly.

It will be something to do, at least.

Something to pass the time.

The middling season.

I was becoming better friends with Grant, slowly and uncertainly. Grant was deeply good and spent his words carefully when approaching any question of God. There was much talk of God in those days, while I tried to sort through what exactly I was doing at St. Paul's, and he wondered about his own denominational home. We went to St. Paul's together a half-dozen times, spent car rides and coffees and walks around campus turning over whether or not we fully believed all of it, these things about salvation and God and grace and sacrament.

Grant taught me to wonder again. If St. Paul's was teaching me in what manner to ask, it was Grant who taught me to ask in the first place.

Sam joined in our little Bible study at Common Grounds around the time Jerry had to stop coming because he was leading things for the youth at his church. Evan, Sam, Grant, and I spent many of our nights occupying a table, studying, talking through stray thoughts that tugged us in so many directions we could never keep track of them all.

I am sharing this because it is a means of collecting evidence.

Evidence that I was beginning to discover wholeness again.

Sam and I. We both had such big questions about God, about the world. We would place them in front of each other just to see what the other would do with them. We were assertive. We were sure. We would press hard on our presuppositions and tease out our deepest hopes.

I was still fractured then, so there was more than once that I thrust my opinion forward like a sword. I cut him. I would apologize eventually, when I realized, and he would accept it. Sam held my anger, my thrashing, my inability to believe that everything in me wasn't broken. He let me spiral and spin out in front of him, and then when I was all done he would speak but one word of peace directly into me.

I should have figured it out the first night, on the bench at Common Grounds: he wasn't going to leave. Somewhere in the midst of that I must have had an inkling; I must have felt the pull of what it would someday be. But maybe I tucked that away for a time, I think, because if I knew then, if I had known too soon, it would ruin me. I would want it too quickly and too desperately and would lose it. Samuel was going to be my best friend, the friend that sticks closer than a brother, the friend who outside of my wife would be the person who knew me better than anyone.

But then?

What I knew was that I was so afraid he would leave. And perhaps more afraid that he would stay.

On Valentine's Day, Addison and I helped Sam put together

something special for his girlfriend Chérie. Between Addison's eye for artistry and my determination to be as helpful as possible, we ended up buying most of what we had already claimed to have for him that he could borrow, putting it together in an ordered, ready-to-go plastic box so that we could hand it off.

He was grateful. Extraordinarily grateful. That's the way with him.

Addison and I went back to her apartment and lay on the couch for a half hour before I finally said aloud, "It's Valentine's Day."

"Right."

"We should do something."

She shifted. "Oh, right! We should have."

"We could go to dinner."

"It's late."

"We could —"

We blinked at each other. I think eventually we watched a movie.

What I remember is bringing the box to Samuel. What I remember is that Addison and I both forgot Valentine's Day.

I'm helping Constance pack her house. I had promised to help her when she told me about the black thing, the shattering of her marriage. She explained how it was hidden, how she should have known, how she had been so easily blinded and so willfully too.

"I guess I have to leave him."

The dishes. They seem to take the most time. We put Chopin on the stereo and wrap them in brown paper and place them into boxes without speaking.

The piano is already gone, the cutting boards put away.

I am silly and young, so when she walks into the other room, I open the wine — the good wine — and pour it all down the sink and fill it with water, re-cork it, and put it back on the wine rack. In the hall, I unscrew some of the light bulbs just enough so that they flicker.

I want it to be miserable for him.

I want it to be like the movies and for there to be this great moment of powerful triumph, all one-liners and easy breaking. I want him to know that he was wrong, for him to feel it to his bones.

When the dishes are all packed, I walk into the living room and she's folding his underwear.

"What are you doing?"

She looks at me with sad, knowing, determined eyes: "The right thing. It's what you do."

When I first began attending St. Paul's, I knew so very little about what it meant to be Episcopalian, let alone liturgical, and what I learned I did mostly by bits and pieces gleaned from a variety of places. My foray into that branch of the Church coincided with the time I was beginning to read saints more consistently, was developing an interest in church history, was becoming versed in the nuance of medieval theological politics. My reason for why water was added to the Communion wine was from a ninth-century theologian named Remigius of Auxerre, who supposed that it was because the wine represented the divinity of Christ and the water the people he had joined himself to, that without the water we would not have been participants in the mystery of the Incarnation. Saint Cyprian says something similar, much earlier, around the third century.

The roof shaped like an overturned ship? Surely, this had something to do with the words of Saint Peter: "In the days of Noah, during the building of the ark, in which a few, that is, eight persons, were saved through water. And baptism, which this prefigured, now saves you—not as a removal of dirt from the body, but as an appeal to God for a good conscience, through the resurrection of Jesus Christ."[29] So too the church building was shaped to remind us by the means we were saved, carried through by the resurrection of Jesus by confession made in baptism that he was Lord, sent out into the world.

Was I certain that these particular explanations were why the Episcopal church I was attending poured water into the wine or why the roof looked like an overturned ship? I wasn't; but, in a strange turn of belief, because that was the reason and significance it held for me, it was as if it didn't matter if it was otherwise.

(There was danger in this, I know, but I believe God kept me safe.)

The issue of knowing and knowability.

In *A Treatise Concerning the Principles of Human Knowledge*, Empiricist philosopher George Berkeley argues that nothing exists, not really, unless it is perceived. Or rather, to say something *is* is to really say *I perceive it*.

The tree falling in the forest. If no one hears, then does the tree exist in the first place? How can we be certain? How do we *know*?

I'm not sure Christian faith works that way. It is why it is called *faith* and not called *knowledge*.

The Creed begins, *I believe*, not *I know*.

What St. Paul's taught me to do was to sit in the midst of its beauty and ask every question I could come up with but not need to have an answer that was intellectually satisfying. I learned to cultivate a habit of wonder.

Did I know how the Communion rite was said to be Body and Blood? Did I know when that change happened? Did I know for certain exactly what that meant?

No.

(And shame on us when we say we do.)

St. Paul's taught me that Tradition commends to us that our questions lead us not to answers but deeper into mystery, deeper into God, and that we look to those gone before us who have been good enough to do their wondering out loud as guiding forces to help us on the journey ahead. They tell us that the tree in that forest does exist, all on its own, but that the only way we'll ever believe it is if we stop toiling with the means of proof.

On Ash Wednesday, I rise early and go to St. Paul's while it is still dark. I meet Constance on the second-to-last row right before the service begins. She's on and off at St. Paul's, slipping between it and the Roman Catholic church most Sundays.

"Something about the Middle Ages," she says once, and that is all she says.

We sit in the parish hall, the narthex is still being renovated, and we wobble on our folding chairs as we read the liturgy of the wandering, of Israel in need of a God that they have turned from again and again. We go forward and Mother Andrea presses her thumb in a dish of ash and then makes the ashen cross upon our foreheads: "Remember you are dust, and to dust you shall return."

We walk out in silence, into the blue dawn.

The vastness of it arrests me, the impossible blue, like the ink of grace spilt across the city. Constance takes a Kleenex and rubs the ashes off herself.

"What are you doing?"

It's my first Ash Wednesday. I want to have done all of the steps, to be seen as one who has done all of the steps. My prayers are automated now, bodied, and I need to carry the sign of them to feel that they have even been prayed in the first place.

She looks at me directly: "There's nothing worse than pious pride."

⋈

For Lent, I give up coffee.

I break the fast on the third day, absentmindedly.

Then I just give up altogether.

I met Tommye Lou Davis that Lent. I was sitting in her office at the top of one of the oldest buildings on campus, talking about a project that Constance had interest in getting off the ground. Tommye Lou was the former chief of staff to the president of Baylor, then an associate professor and associate dean, and would be in a few years the vice president for constituent engagement. If you had a project in mind, you wanted to talk to Tommye Lou.

But as I spoke, Tommye Lou's eyes narrowed.

"You don't want to be telling me about this."

She shifted forward in her chair.

"What's going on underneath all of that? What's going on with you?"

I tell her. I don't know why, but I tell her. I tell her about Avery and The Well and Meredith and Addison, about the novel I wrote and barely finished, about my mother and my father and all my impossible hopes. I tell her all of it for an hour and she just keeps nodding.

Finally, when I am finished, Tommye Lou, who I would learn to call TLD, tapped her finger on the side of her face a few times, took in a deep breath, and said, "You know, I have found in my life that peacefulness is hard won. We have to ask for it so much, or else we might forget we need it in the first place. When was the last time you asked for peace?"

I circled the Eucharistic liturgy in my head, turned it over again and again. Wasn't there something about peace in it? There must be. But she meant daily. I could tell by the way she looked at me.

"It's been a long time."

"Oh yes," she smiled.

Tommye Lou is Southern grace, like that blue dawn on Ash Wednesday. She spreads her words thick around you like protection.

"I think you need to spend a lot more time asking the Lord for peace."

The Lord.

It had been so long since I had heard someone talk about God that way. The definite article, the proclamation in ordinary conversation that we believed God was present in the everyday. She offered to pray for me then, and I said yes, bowing my head and closing my eyes as I had done so many months before, before things faltered and slipped and I wanted not to be too much like what I had been raised with.

Peace. Small, but there.

I would not know this until much later, but Tommye Lou made me okay with being evangelical again.

Near the end of Lent, I'm with Sam one night at Common Grounds after Bible study, and I mention that I want to start going to The Church of No Windows with him. It is where Sam has gone for the past several months. Grant too, and I think that by placing myself more commonly in their lives, I'll better feel that I was keeping my head above water. Sam is happy about this, excited, and says that he hopes I have a good Easter.

I walk back to my dorm in darkness and in silence. I turn over in my head the reason for going, if it's because I think that God will be found there or if it's just about proximity, being near enough to Sam and Grant.

"Because I've lost Addison," I tell the air, perhaps I tell God.

I've known this for a long time. It's been unspoken, but it has been there.

There is nothing so secular that it cannot be sacred.[30]

L'Engle.

I think about that often when I consider the past, when I consider what I was doing things for and what God allowed them to become, sometimes with me, sometimes in spite of me.

Passiontide and Easter.

I am home with my parents, making a point about leaving their table to go to my Episcopalian services. I present this detail to them vulgarly, delighted by how other I am. I miss the point. I make it about *Episcopalian*. I do not make it about church. Worse, I do not make it about God.

The liturgy for Good Friday is haunting. You stand during the reading of the crucifixion account, and when Pilate presents Jesus to the people, you assume their role. Your response is to cry, "Crucify! Crucify! Crucify!" and you are suddenly thousands of years ago, among those gathered lost children of God putting him to death.

The Good Friday liturgy forces you to look at the death for what it is as well as your part in it. It makes Easter sweeter, to realize that we are caught up not only in the mystery of his death but in the power of his resurrection; that we participate in this cataclysmic swing of cosmic time, of God death and God life. And we say that this is the power that lives within us, this God.

When we say we're asking Jesus into our hearts do we know what that means? Do we know the power we're really asking for?

⋈

"How did you stand it? How did you survive?"

Someone asked me that once when I told them a bit of the story of the falling apart.

That semester and a bit of the semester before I was a part of a writer's group that was hosted by Constance before the divorce, before packing up her house. There were about thirteen of us — poets, essayists, short story writers, and aspiring novelists — we'd gather around her dining room table and share our work, critique each other, laugh through big questions about political ideology and economic theory. Someone always brought an article from *The New Yorker* or *The Economist*, and we'd take turns reading it and then picking it apart. A handful of us were always in the kitchen, cooking and baking, while another handful was in the adjoining living room around the piano. Beethoven and Bach early, when we were getting started, and Chopin when we were cleaning up, washing dishes. (To this day I still think of Chopin as dishwashing music.)

Once a week these people were my home. My writing never quite fit there, but that was in part because I had yet to fit into my own writing. Then there was the matter of faith that by and large only Constance and I shared. But there in the midst of the disentanglement of my other life came the rootedness of something new. Those people in that house around that kitchen island and that piano made a new home for me, a place to breathe.

"I don't fit."

Constance looks up at me, mid-chop. "Don't fit?"

"Here, with them. Not really."

"Does that bother you?"

I pause a moment, pick up a knife, take an onion from her pile, and start chopping along with her. "Sometimes."

"Maybe you're not supposed to fit the way you expect to."

I keep chopping. She's still looking at me.

"What?" I finally ask, taking another onion from the pile, beginning to chop again.

"The desert fathers have a saying that nothing is greater or more noble in the kingdom of God than to be content in the very midst of the most ordinary calling."

"What?" I'm frustrated, my blade still working fast.

"Oh, nothing, it just means you really should focus on chopping the onions right now."

And as if to punctuate it, the knife slips in my hand and connects with my thumb, slicing it open.

"Told you." She remarks, almost distantly, before gliding to the other end of the kitchen, pulling down a first aid kit.

That was how I survived. Week to week. Chopping onions to Bach and washing dishes to Chopin.

Selfishly, the worst part of Constance's divorce for me was the loss of that house, those weeks, that piano, and that cutting board.

Content in the very midst of the most ordinary calling.

It's been years, and I am still learning what that means.

I attend The Church of No Windows with Sam and Grant every Sunday in Eastertide until the end of term. I, or sometimes we, go to St. Paul's before, then get coffee together before continuing on. When Sam goes to mentor someone for an hour, Grant and I attend a Sunday school class on the gospel of Luke that within minutes we realize is going to be a challenge.

"The Gospels may be true, but they aren't necessarily fact."

My hand shoots up.

"Yes?"

"I disagree."

"Well—" He is a seminary student, proud of this, proud of all that he has learned. I am proud too, in my own way.

"You can disagree, but I think you'll find that the more you learn about the Bible, the more you'll understand that most of it is myth."

Once, when I was getting coffee out in the foyer, I stopped short when I saw a framed photo of Mary, adorned with a crown. In Roman Catholic tradition, this is the *regina caeli*, the Queen of Heaven. The Church of No Windows was Baptist, or at least played at being so, and I looked over to one of the members of staff and gestured to the image. "What's this doing here?" I was careful not to accuse, but to inquire.

"I don't know. Guess it just looks cool."

The Mother of God. Just looking cool.

"Do you know who it is?" I push, surely this is a mistake.

"Nah," she shrugs. "Probably someone found it in a garage sale and thought it looked good in the space. Must be a saint, though, because she's got a halo."

I blinked several times.

When we were walking out of church, I looked back at Sam and Grant.

"There are no windows in that church. People are just there to hide from God."

I ignored, carefully, the creeping suspicion in me that I was there for the same reason.

So I kept going back.

In Eastertide, around the end of the semester, Antonia, whom I had known from BIC and who had come to the first meeting of The Well, emailed me and asked if we could get coffee to talk about the Great Texts program.

We met at Common Grounds on a muggy, rainy day, sitting out on the covered porch next to the door. She told me that she would be taking Middle Ages in the fall term. I was too, and we exchanged vague pleasantries about sharing that experience together; she wanted to know what she should read before entering the class.

Antonia is faithfulness. The way she moves, the way she tilts her head when she is hearing you and hearing the Spirit.

Antonia was attending The Church of No Windows as well, and we had chatted a few times at church. The church, in which the sanctuary had a pop-art cutout of da Vinci's "Last Supper," was always shrouded in darkness and had a statue of Saint Francis near its entrance that was always wearing a baseball cap. (Which I knocked off his head every time I walked by.) I looked at Antonia and saw something of myself in her, some of the same questions that I had asked.

I made her a list of about twenty-five books, with specific reasons for each. Later she would tell me she only read one or two, that I had been ridiculous, and of course I had been.

What I realize I was doing, now, when I look back on it, was trying to tell her it would be all right. There was something unspoken that had passed between us, a question unasked, and my answers were in the books, in the space they made to sit and let God be and her be and hope that between the two of them there would be something. I was trying to tell her it would be all right.

What will I be?
What will I do with my life?
I return to these questions often.
Two themes in a sonata.
(Was that what the poet Gjertrud Schnackenberg had said? About two themes like railroad tracks approaching each other into infinity?)[31]

The tension of being and doing.

If something *is*, is it because it exists or does it only exist because it can be perceived, that is, perceived by its doing: the noise it makes, the movement, the taste, the smell?

So if I answer what I am, do I necessarily answer what I do?

I wonder.

I wonder if on these two questions the church has built itself toward failure.

The first cause is God.[32]

Aquinas.

The *first cause* is a statement about being. God is the *first*.

I suppose that answers the first question.

I suppose the desert fathers answered the second.

I leave for England near the end of May, just before Pentecost. Between the security checkpoint of the airport and the gate, Addison and I break up.

"I'm not coming back to Baylor."

"All right."

We're on the phone, we talk for ten minutes, we agree it's over, and we don't speak again for the rest of the summer. I tell Sam and Grant about it by an email. I tell them it's fine, that it's for the best, that it would have never worked anyway. I board the plane and don't look back.

"Business or pleasure?"

The person sitting next to me on the flight asks. I swear silently that I am sitting next to someone who likes to talk.

"I'm running away," I say bluntly, then put in headphones before he has a chance to press me for more information.

I realize, somewhere over the Atlantic, that I've told the truth.

I've never felt so alone.

Seven

———◆———

WALLS

Ordinary Time. Summer 2010.

I live on the northeastern shore of England with a pastor and his wife while I serve as an intern for their church. They are kind people, gentle and patient. They find out I have interest in the Middle Ages and nearly every weekend and some weekdays for the next two months take me to ruined abbeys and priories around the country. We hike for miles, and the pastor asks me questions about what I am wondering. I tell him that I am trying to figure out where I fit denominationally, that I am becoming increasingly wary of the tradition I was raised in. This is said carefully, because I don't know what to entrust where and with whom.

"Do you dislike where you come from?" He is not facing me as he asks this, along the path that leads up the hill, where the wildflowers open orange and blushing.

"No." I reply carefully. "I just don't pray there best. The rhythm of written prayers in the liturgical tradition gives me a rooted feeling, and there's something about the reverence of Communion that keeps bringing me back."

I ramble on then about the questions I still have, the question of baptism, of bishops and authority structures, of the line in the liturgy that says we pray for those departed this life in God's faith and fear to continue to grow in their knowledge of God.

The pastor turns around to face me, smiling his eyes into a squint.

"What matters most, I think, is the posture of how you approach and consider it. You Americans tend to be a lot more concerned with defining yourselves than we seem to be. We worry about what for us honors God most in our own lives, so we work together church to church without thinking so much about what we disagree on. The hope is that you're building the kingdom of God together, big and wide and a little wild."

The orange and blushing wildflowers bend in a spurt of wind over the hillside, and I am thinking of Genesis and the Spirit like wind, like breath, hovering over the waters.

Big and wide and a little wild.

I carry those words with me that summer. I carry them to the small Baptist church where I serve and cradle toddlers and whisper against their heads that they have a God who loves them. I carry them on the bus every Wednesday when I ride for an hour to Durham to go to Mass at the cathedral, where, in the room where the Venerable Bede is buried, I am told God loves me by the sign of bread and wine, Body and Blood. I carry them to the small group I begin going to, a smattering of Baptists. And on a night when we passed more wine to each other like passing the peace, when we talked about prostitution and drug overdose, we also talked of Dante's last portion of the *Commedia*, his journey through Paradise, and how in the end what moves us and the world and all things together is the Love, that is God, a little wild, wide, and big.

Sometime that summer, two different people, divided by nearly half a century in age, email me asking that I pray for their discernment with large life choices. I walk the beach one morning with them on my heart, feeling the waves move over my feet as I meter out words for God's direction.

I am staying with friends of my parents in the middle of England, a weekend away from the church I'm serving, and I am a mile up the coast from their property when I decide to turn back.

"And what about you?" I feel God ask.

"What about me?"

"What do you want to do?"

It takes me three steps. "I guess I stopped asking that a while ago."

I got to see Sam and Grant that summer. Sam was doing a summer program at Oxford, and Grant's father was a pilot, so he flew standby to visit. It was near the end of my time in the North, and the pastor and his wife had left for a holiday in Canada, so I spent the last few days of my stay alone with the two who had become my best friends.

Grant arrived first, and as we walked back to the house from the train station, the blue nights of the British summer draped overhead, we talked about baptism. We always seemed to return to that conversation. We kept it going when we were inside, settled, when I walked out into the garden to cut rhubarb to make him a bit of cobbler for a snack. Grant had been baptized as an infant, and he asked if I thought he should be baptized again.

"No."

I turned from the stove, a duck breast in a hot pan slowly letting its fat free from flesh. I think I surprised myself, because it took me a moment to go on.

"Maybe it's more that I think there's a biblical ideal, that there is a Scriptural reason to prefer baptism as following a profession of faith, but that I also take seriously Paul's words that there is but one baptism and Peter's that this one baptism saves us as it was prefigured in the ark of Noah."

Grant tends to ask questions that I have been sitting in for a long time without recognizing I was. When he asks—something about baptism, something about the Eucharist—I realize I have been gathering the pieces for my answer for a long time, slowly bringing together enough strands to begin weaving a response. I've had a lot of accidental boldness with Grant, theological epiphanies I would have otherwise never considered. Grant will ask something like, you are in a remote monastery and a professing, disbelieving beggar comes to you and all you have is the consecrated bread and wine, do you still feed him from it? Or, you believe that it is only right to eat animals that have been ethically killed, your host at a dinner party offers you meat of unknown origin, do you eat it?

When Sam arrived, the three of us went grocery shopping. I bought too much and made too much. I think in the end there were seven courses. It was a night full of laughter and confession and the establishing of something unspoken that was to be the friendship we would continue to share for years.

We talked that night of writing a book someday about the Our Father. I still have the text document where we divided out the lines. Maybe someday we'll write it. I suppose what matters is that we are the sort of friends who want to write a book together about a prayer. You can count on people like that. You end up trusting them in ways that surprise you, that heal you, that are so crystallizing to your hopefulness that you don't notice it's happened until years later, when you write it down, when you see it for what it was and is, and the nostalgia births in you hope once more.

On our last day together, we travel to Lindisfarne, commonly called Holy Isle. We take two trains and a bus to get there. Holy

Isle has a recorded history from the sixth century. Saints Aidan, Cuthbert, Eadfrith, and Eadberht were all at one time connected to the small tidal island, and it is an icon of Celtic Christianity, of the enduring struggle and wildness of the faith in Britain. There's a magic to it, a felt magic. The causeway to get to the island is dry for only a handful of hours in the day, and there are countless stories of tourists trapped on the island because they missed the last bus out when the tide rose. The government reports at least one car every month has to be abandoned on the causeway, despite the warnings.

We walk the beach for a time, wander. I have a plan of sorts, the shadow of one. When we stumble past a very small island off the north coast, lush green against the gray sky, a tall wooden cross high at its point, I say, "There," and we make our way over.

At the foot of that cross, we sit, and I produce a small bottle of red wine, some water, and a bread roll from my backpack. I follow with printed pages for each of us, the Rite I liturgy from the Book of Common Prayer, the Scripture readings a mix of what seems most important to each of us at the time, with all the parts divided among us. We bless the bread and wine for one another, pray the prayers for one another, and offer to one another Communion. We do this quietly, simply, and because it feels true.

When it is over, Grant and I debate what to do with the blessed bread and wine — the beggar and the monastery, in its way. In the end, we settle on pouring the wine out at the foot of the cross to feed the earth, and crumbling and scattering the bread to feed the birds, which I add is asking for the intercession of Saint Francis. We catch the last bus off of the island and arrive back to the house late, exhausted, full and yet emptied.

The next day we go to London together, and Sam and Grant then go on to Oxford. I stay in a hotel near the airport and fly back to America the following day.

I will not feel that still and that at peace again until I meet my wife.

Ordinary Time.
  The season in which something grows.
  Perhaps.
  Maybe time.

By the time I moved back to Baylor for the start of my junior year in August 2010, I had pieced together a few things. I had visited a friend over the summer in St. Andrews, Scotland, who was studying Theology and the Arts at the university there. I was intrigued by the program and started to plan quietly to go there for my graduate work in two years. I had taken up writing a blog too, a poorly formatted repository of stray thoughts and self-aggrandizing theological reflection. If the website's statistics were to be believed, I had a faithful readership of twenty-seven. I started calling myself a blogger.

I moved into a private room of the Honors Residential College and unpacked twenty boxes of books, put in a side table, two bookcases, and, as best as I could, turned the space from dorm into apartment. I was one of only a few upperclassmen who had decided to stay on, and I moved in with the intention to speak to as few people as possible.

I liked my life, my friends, my safety.

The days had turned ordinary. God and the days of wonder had turned ordinary. There was nothing more to do than just to get by and get through.

So I did.

⋈

For my birthday, Sam and Chérie gave me a painting of the veil being torn in the Temple during Christ's crucifixion, which they had painted themselves. The veil's tear reveals a world renewed on the other side, lush green and full and vibrant. It is simple, and it is one of the most important gifts I have ever been given.

"You taught me this." Sam told me when he gave it to me.

"What?"

"About the need for re-creation, about how the world is beautiful, is being made beautiful. And what you will do is spend your life teaching people that."

It's a heavy blessing.

The painting is on my wall now, over where I write these words.

It's a long way from a poster of Virgil.

Constance holds a dinner party in a small apartment she has rented for the semester. She invites all the old faces, the usual group of artists, and we sit around sharing half-wonderings about what the future of our work may or may not be. (There is no Chopin tonight. There is no piano. There are no onions to chop.)

"I'm moving."

She says this when she is handing me the serving dish with the coq au vin. She says it with finality.

I go to her in the kitchen when nearly everyone else starts reading their poetry to one another in the living room. I can hear the cantor lilt drifting into the small room when I ask her to stop wrapping up the leftovers and to look at me.

"What's to say?" she shrugs, an emptiness to the gesture.

"Where will you go?"

"North." And after a moment, "It's time. There's nothing left for me here. Baylor is beautiful, but this season is not. I need to go. I need to be somewhere not here."

She goes back to wrapping the food.

"The Holy Spirit is like wind, Preston. She comes sometimes with a burst, a surprise. One morning you wake up and you know, simply, nothing more than that it's time to go."

Constance paused, looked back over at me, a small and sober smile.

" 'We are spouses when the faithful soul is joined by the Holy Spirit to our Lord Jesus Christ. We are brothers to him when we do the will of the Father who is in heaven. We are mothers when we carry him in our hearts and bodies through a divine love and a pure and sincere conscience, and give birth to him through a holy activity which must shine as an example before others.' "[33]

She turns fully to me.

"The prayer of Saint Francis you weren't yet ready for. It's my gift to you. You may or may not be ready for it now, but it's now yours."

She was gone the next day. She still emails, calls, but I have often thought of Constance as I think of Enoch in Genesis.

She was and then she was not, for God took her.

That semester, Jerry, Antonia, and I, along with Sam, took a course called Masterworks in Art with David Lyle Jeffrey. Masterworks was a Great Texts module that focused on a combination of art history and theological study. We did not only ask questions about how an artistic form took shape, but why it took the shape in the first place. Questions like whether it is heretical to depict God the Father at all or the Holy Spirit as anything other than a dove, since the only Person of the Trinity to have been bodily made known to us as a human is Jesus. Or what do we do with pagan imagery that has been reclaimed for Christian use? What about nudity and the erotic in the arts, or the obsession with death and violence?

Unique to our year, Baylor's Mayborn Museum was hosting a collection of Marc Chagall and Georges Rouault in tandem, so our class convened in one of its lecture halls, and we spent time touring the gallery, which would become the primary focus of one of our papers that term. It's hard to describe David Jeffrey. He is tall, a true Celt, astoundingly brilliant, and impossibly wise. He has a way of looking at you that is itself an entire conversation.

In Masterworks we spent hours discussing the instructions for artistry in the book of Exodus. We learned about the unique word play of God as crafter in Genesis, of the wonder that it was to marvel after the beauty and gracious actions of God in the world, inspiring people to create in turn out of worshipful response.

Near the end of the semester someone asked Dr. Jeffrey what one thing he would want to leave us with, what mattered the most. He looked out at us for a moment, patient as ever, and smiled softly.

"In the Gospel of Luke, right before Jesus walks into the synagogue, unfurls the scroll to a place he looks for, reads from it, says this has been fulfilled in their hearing of those present, before his public ministry begins, he first denounces the craftiness of Satan with this: Man does not live by bread alone, but by every word that proceeds from the mouth of God." There were tears in his eyes.

"So go and do."

And he dismissed us.

It may be my memory playing tricks on me, but I can all but promise you we left in silence.

Sam, Grant, and I attend a Newcomer's Party for St. Paul's, which we understand to be a small dinner for people interested in the church to spend some time with the clergy. We buy a bottle of wine to take as a hosting gift. When we arrive, we realize it's a party where about forty people from the church outnumber the seventeen who are interested in joining. Our bottle of wine is placed somewhere in a corner. We drink cheap wine from red plastic cups. We sit at a table with a couple who describe their spiritual journey as a complicated mess of wanting more but not knowing exactly what it is they wanted.

"And you?"

She looks at me intently.

"You're so young. Why are you here?"

"I wanted to cross myself."

We all laugh.

Did they notice? The flicker in my eyes? The way I passed that off quickly? Did they notice that I was avoiding telling the truth, that I wasn't so sure anymore myself?

Sam spent that Thanksgiving with my family and me. I drove home the same way I had gone the year before, fleeing to Paris, now with my new best friend.

Our lives are circles.

The Sunday of Thanksgiving break was the first Sunday in Advent. I had been going to the Episcopal church near my house most times I was home, but the last time I had passed a sign for an Anglican church, and I mentioned to Sam that we could check it out.

We arrived at HopePointe Anglican Church just as the traditional service was beginning. We didn't know exactly what to make of it at first, a building that was big, bright, loudly welcoming. The inside wall on the way to the worship space was lined with crosses from all over the world in all shapes and sizes. Inside, it resembled a deconstructed gothic cathedral combined with modern accents—stone archways on the stage, a stone table on the dais, candles everywhere, large, modern icons of Christ on the walls. The people were a mix of young and old, gentle in their welcoming and pointed in their greetings.

We sang songs I had sung in youth group at my Baptist church. There was a spirit of peace in the room, suggesting that we were all there for a reason that brought joy to God. They spoke of the need for salvation, of true repentance, and the power of a transformed life. They were a wash of evangelical heart, Anglican spirit, and charismatic sensibility.

For Advent, they had a table to one side of the altar with different sized chisels on it. Some large, some small.

"When you come forward after Communion today," the priest said warmly, "take back with you whatever chisel seems the right size to make room in your heart. Make it your reminder for Advent that we are making room for Jesus, we are cleaning up for Jesus, we are making space for the Almighty to be within us as we expect him to come and abide."

I took the largest chisel I could.

I still have it.

Near the beginning of Advent, I start meeting Jerry near the pub off campus on Monday nights.

We read the letters of Simone Weil together, another book gifted from Constance, who told me once if there was ever a beautiful way to grieve the world, Simone knew how to do it. Over drinks and nachos, we talk baptism, hopefulness, sacraments, the impossibility of our dating lives. Jerry is cautiously bold, holds his words with conviction but offers them to you tentatively.

The action of grace in our hearts is secret and silent.[34]

"Do you ever wonder about your salvation?" He asks me in the midst of discussing Weil in relation to Saint Bonaventure. Weil never thought she could enter the Church, never thought she was quite good enough, and Bonaventure's *Itinerarium* opens with the image of entering the Church, entering the midst of God, underneath the threshold of the bleeding Christ upon the cross. The threshold that Weil said she could not quite step under.

"No." I pause, then reconsider. "You mean, doubt that I am saved?"

"No. Well, maybe that. But I was thinking more about the process of it, what it actually means to say you're saved."

"Oh," I smile wryly, "all the time."

"So, Preston, what does it mean to be saved?" He takes a nacho, holds it coyly, challenging.

"The hell if I know."

We talk about Weil, about how even if she said in words that she could not step under the bleeding cross, that in every way she so obviously was. She yearned for God, reached out for God, stumble-staggered through her words to brush up against God.

"We like being reductive," Jerry murmurs later. "We like saying that all we have to do is recite a prayer or all we have to do is get sprinkled with water or all we have to do ..."

He sighs, stares at the table.

"I'm sure there are exceptions; I'm sure God makes allowances, but when did Jesus's words about wanting us get translated into questions about salvation being nothing more than a ticket to heaven?"

"I think that's why I'm a not-Episcopalian Episcopalian," I answer.

"Something about what the liturgy says about faith, about salvation. Something about how we have to give all of ourselves in those prayers and all of ourselves at that table. Jesus feeds us so that we can go out into the world and feed it in turn—"

"We bring heaven in."

Jerry completes my sentence. I look up. Jerry is still staring at the table when I ask, "What?"

"Thy kingdom come, thy will be done, on earth as it is in heaven. We bring heaven in. That's the point. We are not saved from something, we are saved to something."

"Sounds a lot like works-based faith."

I look at him long and we laugh. We order another round. We talk about the girl he's interested in. But I carry *we bring heaven in* with me, every time I walk toward the altar, every time I walk back and kneel in prayer.

In Advent, with Sam and his girlfriend, I began attending a reading group hosted by the Anglican church plant that was starting in Waco. On Thursday nights we would meet to read *The Screwtape Letters* or another essay from Lewis and ponder it together before ending our time by praying Compline.

It was this circle of people that taught me to be evangelical again in a way that was also liturgical. I had hidden myself from small groups, from Bible studies, from the days of 9:42 and The Well, and had resisted fiercely the temptation to return to that way of being. But during the time for intercessions in the order of Compline, we were stopped and asked what we needed prayer for and one by one people volunteered to pray particularly, sometimes at length, for the need or the rejoicing. Afterward, we prayed through the rest of the service, then had coffee and cake.

It was subtle, the shift in me, but it was felt; the things that needed praying weren't always the written prayers. They were the unwritten ones too. They were the ones that catch in the throat, in the heart.

⋈

Christmastide.

My family is bright and loud and full of life. We attend Hope-Pointe together on Christmas Day, and over brunch afterward my grandmother asks me what the priest meant when he said the bread and wine were the Body and Blood of Jesus.

I say something about John 6.

She asks me if it's transubstantiation. I say no. That's good enough for her.

But what is the Eucharist, if it's not transubstantiation?

I spend a lot of time in this season asking that question.

I am the living bread that came down from heaven. Whoever eats of this bread will live forever; and the bread that I will give for the life of the world is my flesh.[35] Jesus, in the Gospel of John. I realize that I know enough to know what I don't believe it is. But I realize too that I don't know enough to know what I do believe. Maybe that's the point.

We bring heaven in.

It's something about that. Everything must be.

In Epiphany of 2011, I sit in Dr. Jeffrey's office under the pretense of discussing his becoming my thesis director when I say, "I think I'm supposed to abstain from the Eucharist during Lent."

He studies me for some time, then nods gently, "Why?"

Dr. Jeffrey is Anglican. We have circled the question of liturgy before, of sacraments. He has more than once reminded me of the faithfulness of the rhythm of the prayers, of the quietness of this sort of spirituality. He has more than once asked me what I am doing at The Church of No Windows.

"Last week I went to midweek Eucharist at St. Paul's, and after I had received the bread and the wine, the bread clung to the roof of my mouth. I kept trying to get it off, but I couldn't. And I felt God whisper, *If I have given you a word, speak it.* See, for a few weeks now I have wondered if I am supposed to fast from the Eucharist for my mother's healing."

I have told Jeffrey before about my mother, about her disease. I have said that I pray for her—and I do, some days, but not as much as I ought—but this is the first time I speak it with such decided terms: *for her healing.* There's a weight to that.

"I avoided it," I go on, "but I think it's ... well, it's a thing. I can't shake it. I don't trust this part of myself anymore, not since ..."

Jeffrey holds up a hand and nods.

"Throughout the Tradition this has been the practice for several saints when they sought a great movement of God. If you go about this, I'd recommend you devote yourself to a rigorous diet of daily prayer and you get a few people who will walk beside you to pray as well."

I can feel the wafer, once more, against the roof of my mouth.

"Okay."

I buy a dozen prayer books. I put Jeffrey, Grant, Sam, Tommye Lou, Jerry, and a smattering of other people on an email chain for the next thirteen weeks and into Lent. I manage to pray the hours daily for a week. Then I stop. I don't know why exactly, other than laziness, but I stop.

I am invited by a friend to speak at the University of Mary-Hardin Baylor on poetry and the writing process.

I read five poems and then discuss the process of creating them, meditations on the heaviness of being.

"Why do you write?"

Someone in the small audience asks me this, and I shrug. "I have seen something beautiful, and I am looking for a vocabulary that allows me the means to articulate what I have seen."

I believed it then, I believe it now, but when I first said it, it was too practiced, too rehearsed, and what I said sounded loftier and more othering than I would mean now.

"For you."

That's what I should have said.

"I am writing to share with you a vocabulary for the beauty you have seen, so that you can tell me about it, so that you can tell me that God is beautiful."

That's the point.

I hope, at least.

When Anne Lamott came to Baylor, some of the conservative Roman Catholics on campus staged a protest outside of where she was speaking. They peacefully informed me, as I walked into the building, that she had supported euthanasia and abortion. Some of the protesters knew me from classes; they asked how I, as a "good Christian," could support her. I said something rather profane about their ignorance, which startled them, and I walked inside.

In a circle of about thirty chairs, Sam and I sat together while Anne talked about the hardship of being a writer, of wanting so badly to put pen to paper, how there is no money in it, how you hate yourself all the time until you love yourself, how you think you are both brilliant and stupid, how there is nothing better and nothing worse than being a writer.

She spoke about critics, then about loving them in spite of yourself, about how it matters that you can disagree with people and still sit in the same room, about making space for others, about the impossible laughter that is grace. I felt the stir in my spirit, the tensing of my certainty. I had recoiled from one kind of certainty only to chase after another.

"You need a person," she said near the end. "You need a person who will always read you for you. Someone who can say if it's false or if it's true. Someone who can really, really love you enough to call your bluff."

I waited in line with Sam to meet her, and when I did I mentioned something about being one of the people who disagrees with her sometimes but is glad we can sit in the same room. She hugged me, tight, generously, and asked if I was going to be a writer.

"I hope so."

She nodded.

"Do you have a person?"

"He has a person."

Sam said it from behind me. It caught me off guard. I looked back for a moment and then back at Anne, "I have a person."

As we walked outside, past the protesters, I lingered a moment.

"I'm sorry," I told them simply, begrudgingly. "God's peace to you."

When we were far enough away, Sam looked at me sideways, "What was that all about?"

I shook my head. "I don't know anymore."

"You're not the only one who thinks God heard."

"What?"

Sam and I.

"You tell the story about how we met, about how God heard you. He heard me too."

I still struggle to unpack the weight of that.

As an alternative to Baylor's chapel requirement, the Honors Residential College offered a nightly prayer service that was a cobbling together of Compline from the Book of Common Prayer and meditations from the Tradition. On the third floor of the girls' dormitory, in the chapel restored in colonial style, with stained glass that went dark against the night sky, I prayed slow and steady prayers for peaceful sleep and mending to the day.

These are boring prayers.

These are the prayers that you feel like, sometimes, you're just getting through on Sunday so you can finally get out of the pew and go do something at the altar. You have now prayed for *the whole state of Christ's church and the world* so often that you're ready to forgo it a little while, to not care.

But liturgy doesn't work that way.

Liturgy means the work of the people. It means the labor we are to do. Liturgical formation, the work that shapes us, is this: praying the prayers we otherwise wish we could skip over, embodying them, posturing ourselves to be transformed by them, so that we can keep that posture and that work when we walk back out into the world. It is the way we learn the vocabulary of what we have seen, or maybe the promise of what we will see someday again. Maybe for the first time.

We bring heaven in.

In Epiphany, Jerry, Antonia, two others, and I started meeting together at Jerry's house on Wednesday nights for what we would eventually call Fire Circle Wine Nights. We would sit out in the backyard around a fire pit, sipping wine, laughing about our pasts, the ways we pigeonholed God by our own insecurities and wants.

I had started writing short stories, and every week I would read one—about a woman who aborts her baby even though she knows the world is ending in a week; a man so consumed with cracking a code he believes he has found in the Bible that he misses the visitation of God; a young priest and an old priest, locked in struggle over works and grace and works of grace; a group of friends in New York who drink gimlets after the funeral of someone close to them, a drunken and soft portrait of the maddening season of youth and wealth and half-dreams.

Jerry was writing a novel about a college student named Thomas, who suffered from crippling depression and a failed suicide attempt. It was haunting, aching, astute. He'd read us a chapter and we'd give notes. I read a story in turn, and we would wonder together about writing, the practice of it, the way of it, how characters come to you in the middle of the night and tell you they must be written.

Some nights we cooked together, some nights we drank cheap wine that tasted sweet like jam, and other nights we would sit in the stillness, around the fire, and wonder about what was to come next. We circled the topic of *next* often, observed it, the uncomfortable fellow that took up an unseen chair beside us in that circle. In the end, everyone leaves. You know it but you don't. You accept it but you don't. Or maybe that's just me. I've done a lot of leaving already in my life.

Things reached their breaking point at The Church of No Windows on the Sunday we sang a song with Page France's strange, circusesque lyrics about Jesus in the resurrection being dirty, bugs crawling on his body.

I stared blankly at the screen in the sanctuary, stared at the lyrics wide-eyed and disbelieving. Surely not. There were a lot of silly things we had sung in that dark room, but this was something more. The imagery was caustic, gruesome. It was not the gruesome cross, not the gruesome death, but the resurrection made gruesome. It was the glorified and beautiful Christ made into the butt of a joke, a silly thought about the reality of true re-creation, a world that was still messy and decayed even in the glory of being called redeemed. I sat down in the middle of the song while people kept singing. I sat in the darkness and felt panic clutch in my throat.

What was I even doing there anymore?

The sermon was about forgiveness. We ended up hearing about the September 11 attacks. We were told that if Jesus had been the editor of the *New York Times*, the next day he would have run a headline saying we had deserved it, that we had brought it on ourselves for not being gracious to the world. There was a painting afterward, on the screen, which showed Jesus washing the feet of Osama bin Laden. The image was left up as we were invited forward to take Communion, to dip our torn hot dog bun in grape juice and say we had done something holy.

The painting didn't bother me. I believed in radical forgiveness. But the tone of the entire message had been delight in being controversial and offensive, in parading around a dirty resurrected Jesus that said idiotic and self-indulgent things. We were in the darkness because we wanted to hide from God. There were no windows so that we could hide from God.

I stood up, walked past Sam and Grant, and I kept walking until I was in the parking lot, in my car, and with the door closed I sobbed for twenty minutes until Sam and Grant came out and we silently drove back to campus. I never attended a service at that church again.

It was the first Sunday in Lent.

A parenthetical.

> *Walk about Zion, go all around it,*
>   *count its towers,*

consider well its ramparts;
  go through its citadels,
that you may tell the next generation
  that this is God,
our God forever and ever.
  He will be our guide forever.[36]

From the Psalms.

I think about this verse often, about the edges of Zion, the city where God's glory dwells. The command of the psalmist is to walk about it, to go to its edges, to examine all of its facets, its points, the intricacies of its construction. We are to know this city so well that we may pass on to the next generation what we have seen, what they shall go and see for themselves so that they too may pass it on.

I think of the walls of this city, I think of the walls as orthodoxy. The edges of Zion are the minimal foundations of our belief. Our confessions that Christ is Lord or that the resurrection is literal or that in the beginning God created. The side questions, like whether that creation was by six days of literal work or the miracle of theistic evolution, are not the point. The point is that God is creator. The point is that stepping beyond that basic step, that wall, puts us beyond Zion.

My time at The Church of No Windows was spent mostly testing the soundness of the walls that they believed were in place, or perhaps, more accurately, I was walking around the fields of disbelief trying to bring back survivors to edges of the city. And here I stop, because I must admit that what I did most of the time was bring them back to the walls of my own construction. I had built my own small city within Zion, and I was critical of anyone who tested the walls I had made.

Our God is bigger than our walls. God has God's own, but I'm not sure we've found as many of them as we think.

The action of grace in our hearts is secret and silent.

We bring heaven in.

Eight

REPENTANCE

I LEFT THE CHURCH of No Windows, but I did not leave it quietly, I did not leave it well.

That Sunday afternoon I wrote a blog post titled to draw traffic: *The Day I Walked Out of Church*. I detailed every offense, every problem, but assured myself I was doing the right thing because I never once named the church outright. It was God's work to call out the blasphemous, to point out the flawed and graceless.

(And I, gracelessly, went on. Do you see how easy it is? How easy it is to talk ourselves around ourselves, to convict the world long enough that we can avoid convicting our hearts?)

What was I trying to accomplish? Righteousness and aggrandizement sometimes appear too close to distinguish. The post went viral and gathered ten thousand page views within the day. By that point I had a message from the lead pastor of The Church of No Windows asking if we could all have a sit-down and talk.

It had all been building to this. The showdown. The confrontation. (I suppose that's where the problem begins: in the presumption that there are sides and there are sides to be chosen.)

⋈

Antonia and I are standing outside of class, on the pavement that runs across the north lawn. It is windy and cold; it cuts against us like the tearing of the veil in the Temple.

"I understand that you're upset by it, but it wasn't fair."

She is looking at me with a sort of bewilderment. It is the day after I have walked out of the church, and she had been there a row in front of me. She has stopped me on our way into class, with the look of kindness I will eventually learn is the softness of gracious conviction in her.

"You didn't give anyone a chance to process it, to sit with it, to be."

She is intense.

"Whether or not what you wrote was wrong doesn't matter. What matters is that you didn't give them a chance to respond to you in private first. You stopped asking them questions. You stopped treating them like they were people; they were just ideas. But you should have gone to them. And then you go again and again and again and again because that's the way of grace. You keep going back. You keep offering back the chance to have a true conversation."

She shakes her head and turns to walk into class.

"I just think you're better than that."

I remember something, from months before: in class we are discussing the midpoint of Dante's *Paradiso*. Dr. Miner paces at the front of the room when finally he says, "The problem, it seems to me, with most contemporary Christian spirituality is that it is so delighted by its own perspective. We have bought the lie that if everyone is equal, then they are equally right in their perspective on God. Yet there are limiting factors, aspects of unknowability, and while we would say that a surgeon knows more about surgery than a novel writer, we nonetheless throw ourselves into hysterics in trying to deny that a theologian or a member of clergy may know more about God than the surgeon."

He notices how we shift at those words, how they unsettle us.

"Now wait, don't presume too much too soon. What do we mean here by *knowing*? What do we mean when we speak of God in terms of how he is made known?"

He paces a bit more, stops.

"I think Dante is trying to get us to see, by introducing us to all these different people in heaven, how diverse the perspective on God can be and how equally affirming of that perspective we can be, while at the same time suggesting there are deep, core, true things that others are better suited to guide us in."

Dr. Miner looks down the length of the table, to the end where I sit. Is this on purpose? I wonder even now.

"But if this is true, there is a danger greater than anything we normally think of."

He smiles.

"I have suggested that some are more equipped to guide that conversation. Like the surgeon, they are also now more responsible to use that gift well."

Back on the pavement, I call Sam.

"Should I take it down? The post."

"Yes."

"Okay."

I do. And I agree to meet with the lead pastor, a few others, along with Grant and Sam.

"I have to make this right," I tell him later that night.

"You will."

"Well …"

"You will."

⋈

I made dried cherry and dark chocolate chip cookies and brought a half gallon of organic milk, along with cups, plates, and napkins to our meeting at The Church of No Windows. Grant, Sam, and I sat on the couch in the office across from the lead pastor and two associates while I apologized for writing the post and offered peace by means of cookies.

"Why do you keep coming back here?"

It wasn't an unfair question, but I wanted it to be. I wanted to feel righteous still, to feel bold in my words. But I wasn't. I could read on their faces I had wounded them. Rightness no longer mattered—it rarely does when you are unkind. I stumbled over an answer that I can't remember, but I hope it was neither condescending nor presumptive. Eventually we aired our concerns, Sam and Grant spoke their own hearts of uncertainty and reluctance, and in the end we parted ways in gentleness, even if the fragmentation was felt in every step.

As we were walking out that last time, I passed the statue of Saint Francis that stood by the door, still with a cap on his head. I reached my hand out to knock it off, but then stopped myself. It didn't matter anymore. Or it did, but I was no longer the one who could speak the reason into that space.

I was never that person in the first place.

"I'm sorry I couldn't be there, but Ellia was sick again. She's such a little drama queen."

Chris and I sit at Common Grounds, under the watch of Saint Francis by the cash register. We've kept in sporadic contact since my first year at Baylor, since the exchange on the porch talking about women in ministry. She wants to have coffee to talk about what happened at The Church of No Windows, because I learn she was asked to sit in on our meeting originally. The lead pastor knew both of us, knew we were friends, and thought I would hear better and more gently if Chris spoke. She mentions Ellia, her first daughter, with a casualness that always amazes me. Ellia is sick often, in the hospital often, and the way Chris processes it and, in turn, helps you process it, is by turning the worry into tender jokes.

"The brat." I reply without pause. "She really does like hogging the spotlight."

"I read your post. You weren't wrong." Chris draws her legs up and sits cross-legged on the couch, a coffee clutched firmly in her hands.

"You don't think so?"

"Oh, it was graceless and unfair, but you were right." She smiles. "They like not having windows. That's their thing. But you kept trying to make them want windows. That's not exactly kind."

"I guess not."

"I'm preaching there in a few weeks."

"Good."

"Good?" She sits up a bit straighter, "Preston Yancey, have you been changing your mind on me? I thought I could trust you!"

I laugh. "I don't know anymore, Chris." I look at her a long moment, shrug, "I think at this point I just want to hear someone preach a Jesus who is fiercely good and fiercely beautiful. I don't know a lot of people who do that well, but whenever I am with you, that's what I hear. If that's preaching, then that's what I think you're called to."

It happens like that. I say it before I believe it fully.

But I have said it, and that is the beginning of something.

I told my mom about fasting from the Eucharist for her healing, and she held the words of it gently and cautiously. It had coincided with other words from other people, and though she made no particular claim that she believed that come Easter morning she would be healed, she believed there was something in the wind of it all, something whispering the possibility of a thing to be hoped for and in, and so she accepted the fast and the prayer as gifts.

I had enlisted Sam and Grant and Jerry and Jeffrey, added to it Tommye Lou and Constance and a few others. There were twelve in all, and they kept vigil on my mother's behalf for several weeks before Lent and all the way through. Those messages still litter my inbox, the words from Jeffrey the day he lit a candle asking for the intercession of the Virgin, or Tommye Lou, who wrote careful, threaded words about encircling my mother in peace. Constance, with her loud-hearted hopefulness and fierce belief in the impossible made ordinary.

These were my cloud of witnesses, my community of saints. On the days I found it too hard to pray, I knew someone was. On the days I found it too hard to believe miraculous healing could occur, I knew someone did. In the act of recollection I realize that ultimately for me this was the point, that whatever else happened, this was what I needed to understand: faith breathes in community. It suffocates on its own.

Since I stopped going to The Church of No Windows, Lent was spent exclusively at St. Paul's. I met with Father Chuck, the rector, before the first Sunday to explain to him my reason for fasting. Chuck is a tenderhearted man who truly sees people, sees them as they are, and loves them out of that sight. He listened to my explanation carefully and then asked if I had a spiritual director. I said I didn't, and he made a suggestion of one. "To see you through the wilderness of this question," he explained.

He asked me, too, about confirmation, about whether or not I had considered being a full member of the Episcopal Church.

"I think about it," I said softly, "but I'm not ready. I'm also not sure I ever will be. There are too many things that still keep me from it, like my beliefs about baptism. I'm just not sure I can quite fit."

He was silent for a long time, thoughtful.

"Confirmation isn't about agreement, exactly. It's about rooting yourself to a people. You are saying that you are willing to take not only the good from them but also the bad."

I smiled softly and offered a slight shrug, "I guess that's what I'm not ready for."

I meet Barbara in one of the adult Sunday school classrooms at St. Paul's. Barbara is to be my spiritual director, on Father Chuck's recommendation, and we have been casually talking about what that would look like and what it would mean. She reminds me of my grandmothers, of what it means to abide so very long in the midst of wanting God, and I am comforted by the familiarity of it.

"What I am here for," she says, "is to be a listener. I like to think that I'm helping untangle whatever it is you bring to me. Some days you'll have a lot to say, some days you won't have anything. I have only a few rules, that you always come to this space open to the movement of the Spirit and that you will keep yourself open to the possibility of where direction may take you, to at least try."

I nod. "Okay."

She explains our arrangement, then, about the three chairs— one for me, one for her, and the empty one for the Holy Spirit— and tells me I am free to begin whenever I feel comfortable.

I am silent for a few minutes, until I finally say, "I don't trust myself to hear God anymore."

Her eyes widen only slightly.

"You've been sitting in that space for a long time."

"I have."

"Do you know how I know?"

I look at the third chair, the empty chair. I snort.

"God?"

"Well, yes," she smiles and shifts, "but actually I was going to say that it's too practiced. You have been telling people that you don't trust yourself to hear God for a while now. I wonder if it's time to stop doing that."

A moment passes. I tell her about fasting from the Eucharist.

"What does hearing God mean to you?"

"I guess ..." I trail off. "I guess it's that fierceness I used to feel, the knowing of what I am supposed to do."

"When the wafer stuck to the roof of your mouth, did that get your attention?"

"Yes."

"It seems like God knows how to find you when he wants to speak."

We sit in the stillness for a few minutes. She prays for me at the end, schedules me to come back and see her in a month. Outside, in the courtyard on my way out, I pass a statue of Saint Francis, but I don't stop to look at him, to recognize him, because I am more concerned with the business of feeling disquieted than in learning the rhythm of stillness.

At a certain point, Jerry and I stop worrying about whether or not we have something to read and simply meet together on Mondays to talk.

"When are you going to start dating again?" He asked me frankly, but in his usual way, right after he said something otherwise insightful about art in the church.

"I don't know." I find myself saying that a lot these days, and it is not comforting.

"Are you still hung up on Addison?"

"No." I shook my head, "That's long in the past. Besides, I feel too tangled up in myself right now to date. It's unfair to try to make someone responsible for all of your broken pieces — "

"Why do you do that?"

"Do what?"

"Spend so much time talking about how broken you are when you aren't?"

I didn't know what to say, so I finished my drink. He bought me another, and we talked about something else.

"I think it was a piece of construction paper that was glued to another piece of paper, and then they were torn apart, and one side had some bits of the first piece left over on it."

We are sitting around the fire circle on a Wednesday night, Jerry, Antonia, our friends, and I. We are reflecting on our days in youth group, on how they talked to us about sex, about our bodies, about purity.

We have piled high our stories, the horror of what it was like to live through the silliness of it, the shaming of it. At a certain point, our conversation exaggerates, gets unraveled, becomes a riotous critique of the foolishness that comes with sticking two pieces of construction paper together, ripping them apart, and saying that's sex, and you don't want to end up with a lot of other people's bits stuck to you.

But eventually we are quiet, sobered, and someone asks softly, "What do we do to do better?"

We sit a bit straighter in our chairs, looking from the fire up to her.

"It's not enough to disparage it," she pushes. "We have to want better and we have to do better."

None of us really have an answer.

I think about that night a lot.

You are saying that you are willing to take not only the good from them but also the bad.

In addition to fasting from the Eucharist, I give up meat for Lent as well. Except for Sundays and feast days, I forgo flesh as a reminder—at least this is what the Tradition holds—that Christ's flesh was pierced for us. For many, this is a practice only observed on Fridays, the day of the crucifixion, but in my commitment to whatever this fast was supposed to be, I chose to carry it through the whole of Lent.

This wasn't exactly easy. There is a place in Waco called Cupps Diner, and for most of my tenure at Baylor you could only pay with cash. That's the sort of place it is. A small, hole-in-the-wall institution, they make some of the most delicious burgers you could imagine and have been doing so for decades. But they close on Sundays.

On a Friday in March, the twenty-fifth to be exact, Sam and I went to Cupps for lunch, and I ate my first burger in twenty-nine days. My reasoning was perhaps sketchy, but I had worked it out as best I could: the twenty-fifth of March, nine months before Christmas, is the Feast of the Annunciation. I reasoned that the Incarnation was chronologically more significant than the Passion and would therefore trump the usual requirement to fast on the Friday of Lent.

I explained all of this to Sam in particular, who only smiled and nodded because he was just content to eat his burger without making a show of it.

Notice.

In those days I spent a lot of time making a show of the Tradition. To go get a burger on the Feast of the Annunciation was loudly saying that I knew when the feast *was*, not so much that I got to have a burger.

Sam was content with the burger. He knew when the feast was. There was no point in making a show of it.

Lent is a strange season. As Christians, we say our bodies have been made holy in the Incarnation, we have been told that we are made good, made well, formed by a loving Creator. In Episcopal churches we like to focus on this particular part quite a lot. We like to speak of abstract sin, the sin of the community, of racism and sexism and violence, of big abstractions that can occupy us long enough from not really reckoning with that part of the liturgy where we make confession week after week, day after day.

We pray for those sins done in thought and word and deed.

For things done and left undone.

In Lent we focus on sin, we focus on our wandering vagabond hearts. We see the true cost of sin is not as reducible to the brokenness of the world, but that because of it we would nail Jesus to the cross.

We kill God.

That's the line no one wants to look at, that everyone hides from.

There is a painting by Antonio Ciseri called *Ecce Homo*, which is Latin for "Behold the man," the words of Pilate to the Jews in Jerusalem when he presents Jesus to them. The painting is of the room from which Pilate makes the pronouncement, so most of the people assembled look away from you, out to the crowd, Jesus's face turned away, his body bruised and beaten. Only one figure turns away, in the corner. Pilate's wife, who in the Gospel of Matthew is said to have had a dream that caused her to warn her husband that he was to have nothing to do with Jesus. But he ignored her. The Tradition holds that she fled him and later became an itinerant evangelist herself, proclaiming the glory of God and the power of Christ.

Her face, the only one you can fully see, is downcast.

The painting makes you culpable. By its nature, you become one of those who participated in watching God be handed over from the hands of sinners into the hands of sinners for the satisfaction of our appetite for violence.

It does something else too: it makes you want to look away, to be like Pilate's wife and turn, but then you notice the hand, the hand on her elbow from another woman in the audience who is forcing her to stay, or so it seems, Pilate's wife in mid-turn while another clings.

The Scripture says there is none righteous, no, not one.

We are all in that room on that day. Some of us just get to turn away sooner than others.

I drive home alone for Easter Break.

"What do you want from me?" I ask God in the stillness of my car. "What is it that you want, really?"

No answer comes. There are traffic delays, and by the time I make it home, I have missed all the Maundy Thursday services in my area. I watch the Mass on the Catholic television station and hope for the best.

In the darkness that night, as I am falling asleep, I murmur a prayer.

I don't remember what I prayed.

It must not have been that important.

⋈

On Good Friday I attended an evening service at a small Episcopal church near my house. It was full of people, thick with the somber and mournful tones of the day. We walked together around the church, little by little, for the Stations of the Cross. We read the Gospel passages, we remembered the hour in which the veil of the Temple was torn in two. We felt the violence and the weight in our own voices when the liturgy made us culpable, when it had us respond along with the crowd, "Crucify! Crucify!"

I felt it that time in a way I hadn't before, the denial of Communion. At the rail, when I made the sign of abstention over myself, when the priest made the sign of the cross on my forehead and asked God to bring me into life everlasting, it was like a nail into my heart.

The Body passed me by, the Blood as well. I still didn't know what I thought about Communion, about what power it did and did not have, but I knew in that moment what I believed was that regardless of my certainty about it, it was an aspect of the Faith—my faith—that was completely essential.

Christ was made known in the breaking of that bread, in the offering of that cup, and the distance I would feel and fear and declare made me broken was at times only mended by the small fragment of hope that what had been proclaimed in that Eucharist—the Incarnation, death, and resurrection of our Lord—that itself was enough to keep me going, to pray my prayers for me at times.

In the pew, I wept for the impossibility of it all.

"I wish I was there with you."

Sam calls me the evening of Holy Saturday.

"I know. But I think it's good that I do this alone."

My plan is to attend one of the only churches in the area I could find with an Easter Vigil service in the late evening. I don't know the church, so I drive in circles around the area until it's a minute before the service begins so that I don't have to worry about talking to anyone while I'm there. When I walk inside, I find everyone standing in the nave with candles. On Easter Vigil, we process into the darkness with our lights, we enter the darkness of Death with the overcoming light of Christ.

It is a full and beautiful service with a beautiful and full people. They speak triumphantly of the Lord who conquers Sin and Death, laugh and flood the space with light as they declare the day his, Easter Day, rejoicing day. This is the moment I have waited for; the place where I shall take Communion once more.

During the consecration of the bread and the wine, bells are rung.

Bells. In the Tradition, bells were introduced to note the moment of the change, when the bread became Body and the wine became Blood. It makes it too certain; but, when I rise to go forward I am about to receive anyway, in spite of my conviction. I then make the sign for abstention once more.

The priest blesses me, goes on.

After the service I sit in my car staring forward into the darkness of the night.

"I don't know what to trust anymore," I tell the air, perhaps I tell God.

Sam texts me and asks how it went. I answered simply:

"I couldn't do it. Bells."

Easter.

I wake up slowly, without excitement. In another life, at least that's how it feels, this would be the sort of day I rise expectantly, believing that my mother would be healed the moment the Communion cup passed from my hands. Today I am quiet, peaceful. I dress slowly and drive in silence to HopePointe, the church Sam and I attended for Advent a handful of months before.

Joy abounds in the space, surrounds it. The presence of God is thick in the air. I feel, for one of the first times in my life, that I have somewhat of an idea as to what it means in the Old Testament when it says that God causes God's Name to dwell in a space. In that sanctuary I sense God, know that nearness. It is something in the way of these people, the way they blend the oldest things with the fresh desire to see God and to have God seen. They speak of God in near terms, in proximate words, and this is that great comfort of the evangelical tradition, that it believes God is intimately ours and intimately present. But they weigh it, too, against the larger and wider way of doing things, and they speak of God as holy and other, as the one who makes a space for us to come to God, and that somehow in tandem holds all of God without confining God.

I realize, so softly that it does not catch up with me until years later, that I am home.

At the rail, the woman I eventually will know as Deacon Lisa places a shard of broken wafer into my hand and says, "My brother, this is the Body of Christ, broken for you," then follows the cup. Nothing happens when I consume it, nothing radical anyway. I cross myself and murmur, "Amen," rise, and make my way to the side chapel, where I kneel again and pray.

I feel in that moment that all of those who have been praying alongside me are also at that rail, I feel them kneeling there, receiving from the same Lord, the same Communion. I have a moment of clarity in which I realize that ultimately bells rung or unrung do not matter when compared to the impossible mercy that is the God who is willing to die so that we may be united with God in order to live, that this sign is made known to us in the breaking of the bread and the sharing of the cup, and that in the end of all things is God, and we are, in all times and places, caught up into that great and unconscionable mystery.

I went to church with my parents after and, once home, by my mother's request, we had Communion together. Bread and grape juice. The Baptist way. My father blesses the elements and then hands them to us. We eat. We drink. I cross myself, they bow their heads.

My mother says that what she was given was a reaffirmation to hold fast in hope, that healing is coming. She feels the certain peacefulness of that. I nod. Surprising myself. When I email everyone who had been praying that afternoon, Constance is the first to respond.

"It is enough," she writes. "God is enough."

There is a Jewish prayer of which I am particularly fond on the days when I circle back into myself, on the days when I don't believe that God has promised.

And so, O Lord our God, grant thy awe to all thy works,
and thy dread over all thou hast created,
that all thy works may fear thee,
and all who have been created prostrate themselves
*   before thee,*
and for one union
to do thy will with a whole heart.
For we know, O Lord our God,
that the kingdom is thine,
that power rests with thee,

that might is in thy right hand,
and that thy name is awesome over all thou hast created.[37]

I suppose there was a sort of healing, in the end.

I was freed for a time from my need to fit theology into tidy categories and the people along with it.

And another thing.

I emailed Avery and Isabelle and asked their forgiveness for the ways in which I must have been unkind, must have been unfair, for things done and undone. Isabelle wrote back saying she had forgiven me a long time ago.

I never heard from Avery.

There was a lot of eating during those days, in the stretch of Lent and Eastertide. I spent most of my time with Grant and Sam around food, around tables, where we would offer back and forth to one another the questions that wove and bound us.

Grant. I wasn't wrong the first time I said he looked like a rector. He is pastoral, wise, and has a way of hoping for you when you forget to hope for yourself. (Sam is like that too, but with joy more than hope.) I asked Grant once about the humanity of Jesus, about what we are supposed to do with the God who died. He told me we're not supposed to do anything but sit in the tension of the question.

Sitting in the tension. I sometimes wonder if that's how I'll spend the rest of my life.

In a slight subversion of the usual system, Sam, Chérie, and I took Dr. Jeffrey's freshman-year seminar called Literary Bible that semester as juniors. Literary Bible is a rite of passage. Dr. Jeffrey carefully introduces the biblical text with the simple question of considering it within the genres that it was written. Not every book in the Bible is written in the same way. The point of Genesis, for instance, is not the point of Luke. One explicitly states that it seeks to give a historical account of events, while the other makes no claims to historicity, at least in the beginning, and is rather telling a story of how to see the creation as uniquely and completely God's.

"There is a tendency," Jeffrey tells us once, "to want the Bible to be tidy, neat, tamed. But if the Bible is God's, it cannot be those things, because we do not serve a God who is content to conform to our expectations of tidiness, neatness, and is anything but tame."

He wanted us to hear the beauty of Scripture, the rhythms of it, so our usual reading was large chunks of the text with four to five poems from different centuries that served as a commentary or exegesis on the passages we had studied. When someone asked how the symbolism could be so heavy in a particular portion of the gospel while still being a historical account, he answered, "Saint Augustine says that God is an author who writes with people and events the way a writer would use words and sentences."

"The Tradition as a whole teaches us one thing," he said once, near the middle of term, "that if we do not have our footing in the language of the Bible, our prayers suffer, our imaginations suffer, our very way of seeing the world suffers. As a whole, in harmony with itself, Scripture gives us a way of seeing. It invites us to behold the beautiful of the creation."

I start wondering about Confirmation.

Episcopalians are not Anglicans, or is it that Anglicans are not Episcopalians?

This was easier when I was Baptist, when it was just about

joining the people you liked the best and agreed with the most. The Eucharist changes all of that. You're all suddenly at the same Table and you have to ask less about rightness and more about where best you pray. I realize that I am starting to think of myself as not Baptist.

I realize I haven't been Baptist for a long time.

Jeffrey cheekily asks me what I want to be when I grow up.

"I think what I really want to do is write books."

He nods. We are discussing my thesis and what exactly it should be. We are weighing a study on mimetic violence in myth, on ancient commentaries on the Gospel of Matthew, on a theological study of Simone Weil.

"What if," he muses, looking at me directly, "what if you did a more creative project? What if you took some of the parables of Christ and exegeted them in the style of the ancient fathers and the medievals? That's where your heart really lies, doesn't it? In Scripture?"

"Yes."

He smiles.

"Are you sure you're supposed to go to graduate school? You're not supposed to sit on a rock somewhere and write books?"

"I'm not sure of anything anymore."

He laughs, loud and hearty.

"Good. God can show you the rest in due time."

"I think I can trust my hearing of God again."

Barbara studies me a long time before speaking, "You do?"

"Yes."

"What does that look like?"

"It's hard to describe, it's just this sense of presence."

She nods.

"So long as what you hear from God looks and sounds like Jesus, then it is true."

I nod, because I understand. I don't even realize how much I don't.

"It's confusing at times. There's a lot of standing up and sitting down and kneeling and bowing and sometimes you cross yourself ..."

I am explaining St. Paul's to Antonia on our way there. She has recently decided to walk away from The Church of No Windows herself, to seek out newness and other, and I mention that she could tag along sometime if she wanted to see what liturgical church was like.

I spend the entire service nervous that it will seem too Roman Catholic or that there will be too many stand-up-sit-down motions. But Antonia takes it in silently, watches it unfold, and when we go up for Communion, she receives without hesitation.

I go to lunch with Sam and Grant afterward, and since it's the end of the semester, Antonia and I don't talk about church again before the summer break.

On the last day of classes my junior year, I return to The Church of No Windows one last time. I find the lead pastor in his office and I apologize. I apologize for the unfairness of wanting him to be someone he isn't, of trying to be the Holy Spirit for him.

He thanks me. We leave it at that.

On my way out I notice the statue of Saint Francis. He no longer has a hat on his head.

⋈

"You'll meet her when you least expect it," Jerry once said. "She has to be something special to handle all of you."

I blink at him.

"What does that mean?"

"You'll see."

And he smirked.

I leave Baylor without much pretense. It has been a year of peaceful transition. I don't much want to dwell on anything more than that. I go home, unpack, and abide. The plan is that I will work for my father for a time and then go back to England. I have no grand designs. I have no plans other than to read for my thesis and contemplate graduate school.

In late May, early June, I go with my parents to Phoenix. I stay with them a few days before heading home alone. I am in the airport. My phone buzzes and a Facebook message pops up from someone who reads my blog, who found me through a mutual friend, who had found me originally from a fellow blogger. This message casually introduces me to this other blogger, this young woman, who writes in a similar style and who I may be interested in.

While I'm boarding the plane to head home, I click the blog link and read through the entries I find there. My breath catches and I try to steady myself. The words lilt, delicate, but sure. She writes like she knows someone is watching, like she is showing off just a bit but it's so you'll pay attention. She's teaching you but you don't mind you're being taught. And then I see a picture of her, the way her smile arcs, the way she looks into the camera like she sees through to you, truly sees you, and is asking whether or not you will bother to see her back.

I am on the plane when I know who she is. I can feel it flow through me, like the Voice I thought I used to hear so often but now missed so much. I am arrested by her, consumed. I am suddenly aware of how incomplete I am, the measure of distance between myself and this person who I have never met and yet I feel I have always known.

When I land, I text Sam with a link to her blog and the simple message: *I think I'm going to marry her.*

Her name is Hilary. In full, Hilary Joan.

Which means, I would come to learn, in the Latin and the Hebrew taken together, *Cheerful gift of God.*

It is the Sunday of Pentecost.

Nine

———— ◆ ————

GRACE

WE ARE BACK TO where all of this began, with Jesus on the couch.
Well nearly.

There is the summer to account for—Ordinary Time, always
Ordinary Time—and a bit of the transition back to Baylor and
what came the night before Jesus and the Silence and the couch
and the doubt.

But before all of that I want to repeat Barbara's words, the
words she commissioned me with at the beginning: "Here is the
table before you. This is the wilderness. You have arrived somewhere. God has brought you to somewhere. He said it would be
about trust, and, you see, it is. You're in this somewhere space, this
wilderness space. Now, go have a look around."

That's the point of all this, I think.

I went and had a look around. I circled back to see it all again,
and now I will circle back on that time, the silence, and retell it.

Maybe this time more truthfully.

Maybe this time more trustingly.

⋈

Summer 2011. Ordinary Time.

Hilary and I begin a long series of Facebook message exchanges, back and forth with mounting length with each click of Send. She lives in Massachusetts, too far to drive for any rational reason, though I consider it often. We are curious about one another, about what we believe and want and hope for. There are too many questions to ever answer fully, or well, because they are about liberal arts education and sacraments and whether or not Chuck and Blair were really supposed to be together on *Gossip Girl*.

There is a frenzy to the responses, a hopefulness that passes between us that is nearly palpable, even across digital space. She is a poet and a writer, wants to spend her life sowing graciousness in people. She has read more books than I have, but took time to live in Paris and Washington, D.C., speaks political theory like she speaks her favorite meals from small villages in Italy I have never heard of. And in all this she is humble. She offers it forward as a thing to be shared, a place for me to enter and sit beside her and touch and feel and know, too, the beauty she has seen.

A month into our exchanges I suggest a digital date, a Skype conversation where we can finally "meet" one another.

She says yes.

Beforehand, Sam calls me.

"Are you going to marry this girl?"

"I think. Maybe."

"Yeah."

"What?"

"You know exactly what."

I pause.

"Yeah."

Hilary and I Skype for five hours. What begins at a bistro near my house turns into me calling her from my car when the bistro closes to me calling her from my room when my parents are concerned that I have been sitting in our driveway for the past hour and a half. I notice again, not for the first time, how unspeakably beautiful she is. Her eyes capture you, and there's something in the corners of her mouth when she smiles, like she's keeping score of the verbal exchanges and you desperately want to ask her who is winning.

When it is well past midnight, we say good night.

I lie awake for hours, thinking about her. I think about how good she is, how impossibly kind, the beauty that pervades the air she moves through. I am completely in love with her.

I am completely terrified my brokenness will hurt her.

I tell her there is no spark.

That is, I lie.

I lie to Hilary and to Sam.

I message Hilary to tell her that we really shouldn't be anything more than friends, because there is no spark.

I text Sam and tell him that it really didn't work out because there was no spark.

Sam calls me and I ignore it.

He texts me and asks if I'm sure.

He knows. He always knows.

I lie again and say that I am.

"Why do you do that?"

"Do what?"

"Spend so much time talking about how broken you are, when you aren't?"

Near the end of the summer, I went back to England. Like the summer before, my father had organized a team of students who went over to work with churches, and I served as a liaison for one of the groups with the local community. Those were quiet days. Hilary and I weren't speaking. She was, as well she should have been, furious with me. Sam had asked before I left if I was sure, and again I lied to him, saying that I was. "There's just nothing there," I pressed, then reminded him I was getting on a plane and would have to turn my phone off.

Near the end of the trip, my father and I took the train from London and went up into Scotland and to St. Andrews so that he could get a sense of the town and why I wanted to go there. We invited my friend, whom I had spent brief time with the summer before, to come up to dinner and talk about the masters of letters and PhD programs. I was leaning toward Scripture and Theology, a degree I thought would have a lot more practical application in terms of what I wanted to do in the world, which was still a vague plan of something to do with God and lay people and talking about things like faith well. But the conversation continued to turn more artistic, every turn, and by the end of dinner I was wondering if what I really should be doing was getting the same degree that she had, in Theology, Imagination, and the Arts. The program was focused on the question of how art helps us or hinders us in engaging God, questions the possibility of the sacramentality, of the thin places in which heaven is brought in, of all things when seen in certain ways.

My father left us so he could go Skype my mother, and my friend and I kept talking about the future, about what it would mean to get a degree in art and theology, which sounded as realistically applicable as my soon-to-be-completed undergraduate major in books. She only laughed and asked what I wanted to do with my life most, and when I said something about writing and hopefulness and seeing the beautiful, she looked at me a long time.

"That's not Scripture and Theology," I finally said. "I will always love those, but my heart is in the arts that flow from them."

She nodded, resolutely.

After she left, I went back up to the hotel room and walked in on my father still talking to my mother.

"I'm going to St. Andrews for theology and arts," I announced.

"We know," my mother said through the computer screen. "Your father and I just prayed about it."

"Well, okay."

"Okay," they both said.

And it was as simple as that. Peace came as quickly as that.

Notice.

A different kind of hearing.

This was a question of peacefulness.

No Voice. No loudness.

Quiet.

The slightest and most gentle tap in one direction, that perhaps the will of God is found in the midst of, not before, the setting out on the journey.

Of the original Fire Circle, only Jerry, Antonia, and I returned to Baylor in the autumn of 2011. The others and Jerry had graduated, the former off to graduate school and Jerry attending a seminary near Baylor, which Antonia and I questioned him about from time to time. Jerry was too clever for it, we thought, and he had too much to give. But he seemed happy, so we let our concern fall fairly quickly by the wayside.

Our lives had gotten busier. Antonia and I were in our senior year, Jerry was as overcommitted as ever. We adjusted our usual way of seeing each other to the mornings and began a tradition affectionately called Old Lady Brunch. We'd meet each other at the café on the north side of town and over biscuits and pancakes and coffee that was never quite strong enough, spilled out the usual.

We had been changing spiritually. Jerry wasn't quite sure anymore that he was a Calvinist, not in the usual sense, and Antonia had been going to St. Paul's. She had read Lauren Winner's memoir of coming to the faith, *Girl Meets God*, and had fallen in love with the Episcopalians.

"I don't think I could ever be one," she said confidently, "but I mean … it's all the things. It's what I have been looking for, I think. At least for now."

I told her I thought she would become ordained as an Episcopal priest someday. Jerry agreed. She told us both we were idiots.

"I get you," I said casually, picking up my coffee, "I don't think I could ever be confirmed either. It's just where I pray best."

We talked then about the rightness of that sort of thinking, of if we were doing a disservice somehow to the Tradition as a whole, picking the parts we liked without taking on the parts that made us uncomfortable but were perhaps supposed to. Our major of books had taught us to ask questions and to ask them often. But we realized that its limitation came in the need for those questions to remain open-ended when, in the modern world, it was not easy to find church communities that preferred the uncertainty of those questions over the quick and ready answers they were fond of giving.

"But there are some things," Jerry pressed, "that we have to hold on to, that we have to say we're willing to stake a claim for."

"The walls of Zion," I replied, nodding.

Antonia breathed deep, smoothed her hands on the table before her, grace rolling off the motion. "Yes. But." She smiled. "Sometimes it's hard to know exactly what the walls are."

"Yes." I shifted in the booth. "And when you find them, what do you do with them if other people don't want to go exploring or to keep safe?"

Jerry shook his head, "There's nothing safe about it."

"I suppose not."

"Which is the point." Antonia concluded.

That semester, Antonia and I take the eighteenth- and nineteenth-century module for Great Texts. We read Arnold, Goethe, Austen, Dostoyevsky, Wollstonecraft, Edwards, and some of the romantics. When we read Goethe's *Faust*, we linger over the opening scene, in which Faust is translating John 1:1 and uses every word he can think of to translate with and finally settles on *in the beginning was the deed*.

The deed.

Not the Word. The deed.

Jesus is not seen as the word of God that the prophet Isaiah says shall go forth and not return void until it has accomplished all it was sent to do, but a single action, a doing, an isolated event with definite start and finish.

Antonia and I talk about this often, about the subtlety of the shift, of the writings that come before that speak of an enchanted world in which God pervades, saturates, makes Godself abundantly present. This against the later writings, when God must be sought out, when God is the unexpected visitor into a space, when our prayers turn to things like, "We invite you into this space, God," which is one of the most ridiculous things to say, if you think about it, because the point of Pentecost is the declaration that the earth is the Lord's and the fullness thereof.

It happens subtly, but it happens. We get comfortable thinking of the Bible as a past thing, something that lives only in its context and time period and that one lie snares us all. Jesus was, not is. Jesus had, not has. Jesus went, not goes.

Hence the confusion at Christmas: joy to the world, the Lord *is* come. Not has come. *Is* come. Jesus is come into the world. Jesus is ever and always coming into the world. And he sends us forth in the same way. In the Great Commission, the word *go* is literally *as you go*. He sends us out, so that as we go we make disciples.

In the beginning was the word. Not the deed. But how often do we think about that? Rightfully and fully? How often do we wish Jesus would stay in the Bible, where he belongs?

I think that's how I lived in those days.

It was safer that way.

That year, Grant had moved off campus to his own apartment, and Sam and I would go to his house for dinner on Sunday nights. Grant and I would cook while Sam uncorked a bottle, and we settled into our rhythms together, though different now that we spent more time apart. We did not have Sunday in common anymore. Grant was going to a beautiful church in Waco that combined Baptist sensibility with liturgical practice, and Sam had started to go to the same church as Chérie, who would become his fiancée within the year. I had given up trying to find a church to go to other than St. Paul's and had settled comfortably into my maybe-Episcopalian spirituality.

"What about Hilary?" Sam asked once, while he was pouring our drinks.

"There was no spark," I repeat the lie, slicing through an onion, which has me thinking of Constance and Chopin.

"That's not a reason," Grant says patiently, not looking up from the venison he's searing over the stove.

After taking a class in Christian ethics, Grant committed to only eating animals that were humanely killed. It had changed the tenor of our Sunday nights, with a lot more vegetables showing up than had used to. He was, as always, careful about it, though. He believed the fulfillment of Christ's words in sending out the seventy was that if he was in the home of someone who offered him meat not ethically slaughtered and there would be offense not to take it, he would still eat because it was more important to show graciousness to the host than to hold his own conviction over others. I think about this often, when I am in a church that doesn't believe in crossing themselves or doesn't feel comfortable when people bow. I think about what it means truly to submit, in the Christian sense, to one another.

I think all of this to avoid his remark about it not being a reason.

I just keep slicing the onions and eventually the conversation moves on.

We are sitting at the high tables in the back of Common Grounds, Jerry and I. Something exciting has happened, though I don't recall what now, and I am gushing all of the joy and the breathlessness of it in a frenzy when I realize that he is too quiet. I ask him what's wrong, and he tells me, slowly, carefully, and though I hear him correctly the first time, I make him repeat it twice so that I am sure.

"It is, at least, depression." He says it slow. "But maybe more."

He spills it out between us, a darkness that I feared could end up being his but I had always hoped wasn't. It pours out on the table between us, keeps flowing, and all my words that I try to dam the spill are nothing compared to the flood, and it pours out, pours over, and nothing I do will keep it all together.

"It's what we walk through," he says at the end, when I fight hard not to cry in front of him. "Today is just another day."

I am thinking of Joan Didion. How she says it is always described like this, how we fixate on the ordinariness of the day when the tragedy visits us. Comes in, shadow and shade, sweeps in on the otherwise perfectly ordinary day.

We call Antonia. That night, we eat in a loud, brash Mexican restaurant downtown. We toast to something, though what it is now I can't recall. There is a woman outside the restaurant who is homeless and asks us for food. We order her a meal.

Sometimes the Eucharist is given for the sake of asking for divine healing.

The drinks and the ordered meal. It was a eucharist of a kind.

We assemble in the small stone chapel with the large wooden cross that hangs under the porthole window through which the afternoon sun pours through. There aren't enough seats, and more than twenty of us stand arrayed in the back, close enough to one another to feel the weights that each of us have carried the past week. Close enough to help shoulder them a bit too. We are all in a way foreigners here, attending a service instituted by an Anglican Communion mission being held in the chapel of a Baptist church, a patchwork congregation of Methodists, Presbyterians, a Pentecostal or two, Bapto-Anglicans, and everyone in between.

But we have come here to be united in this: the baptism of a child who has declared Christ to be her Lord and Savior.

There aren't enough booklets with the liturgy and the hymns printed on them, so we share. We share with strangers, but who are nonetheless familiar, for they are here with us for the same reason, and this is our unity.

(This is the great mystery, that we are all brothers and sisters and each service, each time we gather together, we gather like a family having a reunion.)

The priest explains the service: we read the Scripture; we share prayers of thanksgiving; the candidate for baptism is asked if she affirms those things common in our faith; she is taken to the font to be fully immersed in the waters; we as a whole, as a family, with our new sister, share the Eucharist.

Some are familiar with these things—Sam, Grant, and I, among others—some find them strange and new. But together we fumble our way along the liturgy, some of us crossing ourselves, some of us bowing, some keeping silent, some repeating, and we find somewhere in the midst of these diverse responses that common note of prayer. This note that is part of making us into the notes of the Song.

We follow the priest and our sister-to-be out of the chapel and to the font. There the water is blessed; we too are reminded of the vows we have made to our Christ; we affirm them again; we affirm that we shall, diverse as we are, watch over this sister in prayer and hope. Upon her profession of faith, she is submerged in the name of the Father, the Son, and the Holy Ghost.

And we erupt in applause.

Our applause rips through the fabric of the place where we find ourselves, bursts forth and draws heaven just a bit closer than it was before, brings it in—Jerry, I am thinking of Jerry and the waters that spilled out on that table and now splash up at this baptism. A sister has been welcomed into the family, and there is no need to quibble over theologies or styles or methods here, for this is glory and grace enough.

We return to the stone chapel, to the wooden cross, to the resplendent sun pouring in.

We quietly walk forward and receive the Body and Blood.

Some do not and stay seated, some go forward and are blessed. Some see the sacrament in one way, some another. What matters is that the family is together and the family is celebrating. Celebrating under the wooden cross, bathed in the endless light.

On this day we gathered together to celebrate this baptism. I am thinking of Jerry and thinking of the pain, of the wound. And on this day, of all days. It is the day of the mournful. But there was no better way to remember, or perhaps to redeem, than this.

It is September 11, 2011.

⋈

I started reading Madeleine L'Engle's *Walking on Water*. L'Engle describes art as a form of annunciation and incarnation. The Spirit comes to someone and tells them they are to create, and in the action of creating, they are partnered with by God, and what comes forth, if it is true, is both of that person and of God.

"And what does that have to do with your alleged brokenness?" Barbara asks me once, in the circle of three chairs.

"I'm not sure it has anything to do with it. I've just been thinking about it a lot when it comes to how I want to be a writer."

She tilts her head, "But being a writer is a giving task; it reaches into you and pulls all of you out and hands all of you over."

"And?"

"And how are you going to do any of that if you don't believe that God is already partnering with you in your life? Has already made the annunciation, is in the midst of realizing the incarnation that he has given for you to do."

"I don't know what you mean."

"You, Preston," and she points softly toward me, "you are the work of art that God wants to partner with you to work on right now. A broken vessel cannot control how it pours out. But you are not broken; you are simply afraid that you are. So you resist being filled."

That is how I ended up with Jesus on the couch: a conversation about my fear that I was broken when I wasn't.

The day I left Barbara was the same day I drove up to Austin for a belated celebration of my birthday thrown by SJ, who had moved to be closer to the arts community but was commuting to Baylor to keep teaching her classes. At a lazy dinner in the autumn night under the light-strung trees of the French bistro, a handful

of us talked about the year past, the hopes of the future, and what
may or may not be to come for me. I read a short story about two
people who had been desperately in love and whose untangled
romance ended on Pentecost.

SJ patiently heard the tale before she fixed her gaze on me,
"You're not over someone."

"What?"

"That story is about you and someone else. Who is it?"

I am nervous so it comes quickly, too quickly, and it is a lie.
"Addison."

SJ's eyes narrow slightly, and I can't tell if she believes me or if
she knows that this is something I have to find out for myself, the
hard way. "Then you should call her."

"Maybe."

There is a moment, long and uncomfortable, and then it passes.

I call Addison that night. I tell her I have been thinking about
her, which is true enough but is not exactly true. She has been
thinking about me. We wonder if we should give it another try.
She's back on the coast. She is well. She is happy, but she misses
me. I say I miss her, because it is the thing you say.

The next morning, I go over to SJ's and am sitting on the couch
of her apartment before a group of us head to brunch when I open
my Bible and read the passage in Luke.

And then he is there, beside me.

I told you before I tried to make small talk, and I did, because
what I did not want to do was to talk about Addison or Hilary or
my fear of brokenness.

It's going to be about trust with you.

And then he is gone.

And it is felt. The goneness is felt. Something leaves me. Something is taken from me. And all that is left is a silence so loud, I
think it will make me deaf.

⋈

You have already read this.

You have already traveled this time of silence.

The story to tell now is the story of what happened between those other stories.

It is an incomplete tale without the other moments.

Pinpoints.

Lights along the way, promising a greater light in the end.

Can God make a table in the wilderness?

God can. God does.

But sometimes it takes a while to see it.

Sometimes you're so hungry and complain about your hunger for so long, you don't see how full the table is before you, has been before, has always been before you.

"Is it depression?"

Sam asked me this on the bench outside our dormitory. He had moved in to the Honors Residential College for our last year and lived just down the hall from me. It has been a month or so since Jesus left, and I have been slow and sluggish and bitter, dejected from the world around me.

"No, I don't think so."

But I wonder.

There are mornings when I wake up and the measure it would take for me to set a foot out of my bed onto the floor seems impossible. Scripture and prayer seem pointless. God, as concept, let alone as intimate, is this great and impossible Other removed from the landscape of my heart, even though I know God's still lurking and hanging around.

How did it happen? So suddenly and so fast. The God who I

thought I knew that night we were going to start a church, or when the wafer stuck to the roof of my mouth, where was that God? Where was the God of the closeness? The comforter?

"I'm numb." I confess to Sam, and he murmurs recognition.

I do most things, in those days, numbly. Apathetically.

I do them because they need to be done.

Addison and I last for a month and a half of long distance phone calls and Skype before we both realize there was nothing left between us and very likely never was to begin with. There was a safety, though, in having that relationship, and it meant that when Hilary reached out to me again—her anger had passed, to a point—I felt as though we could talk without the risk of the weight of my brokenness being too much for her. Though it's telling, in all of our exchanges I mention Addison three times in the space of the entire time I was allegedly back together with her and every time Hilary ignored it.

After Addison and I broke up, I pretended to be too busy with school, graduate school applications, thesis writing, and friends to keep up a consistent conversation with Hilary. I would relish every message she sent me, lengthy and full of beauty and tenderness, but then would take days and weeks to respond myself.

All the while, I was turning over the question of silence, of the empty space in my heart.

I had friends who had walked through seasons of doubt, who had disbelieved in God or the church. This was not that. I felt betrayed. I had done all of the things you were supposed to do. I had prayed the prayers, read my Bible, followed the prompting little by little in the way I believed God had shown me I was to go.

And my reward was silence. Nothingness. A feeling of absence.

I never once doubted God. I doubted myself. All the time.

I hadn't done enough. I hadn't been enough. I hadn't prayed or read or whatever enough.

I can see it now, more clearly, that this had a lot to do with how I responded to Hilary. But I didn't want to see that then.

I'm not sure I want to see it now.

"What did we not give you when you were growing up? Did we not tell you enough that God was always with you?"

My mother asks me this much later, when I read her the first chapter of this book.

"It's not like that," I say after a long pause. "It's not that simple. I never lost belief that God was with me. It's that he was with me but wasn't, was there but wasn't, was present but was absent. It's hard to describe. I guess." I pause again. "I guess it's just that the *feeling* of God was gone. I didn't feel God anymore, that happy, joyful sense that God has made the whole of the world God's. I know it intellectually, but I don't feel it."

She looks up at me, "That last bit. You said it in the present tense."

I smile softly. "Yeah."

I spent most of my free time at Common Grounds that year, along with most of my money. I would go for hours at a time, under the watch of Saint Francis, and pore over my books and computer, slowly working my thesis into some semblance of good work.

I took a directed readings course with Dr. Miner that semester, and we met every Thursday for coffee to discuss the first thirteen questions of Saint Thomas Aquinas's *Summa Theologica*. They were the questions on God's greatness, God's otherness, and more than once Dr. Miner asked if I was all right as we slowly worked our way through the responses that reinforced how distant and beyond God was from us.

"Yes," I said every time, and smiled. "Just thinking about how far away God can be."

(The next semester, we would meet again for the same purpose, but Dr. Miner would choose the questions about Christ, about the Incarnation, about how close and intimate and present God is with us. It wasn't subtle, but it was kind.)

All around me, a tangle of people, some from The Church of No Windows, some from The Church of the Flaming Spirit, and everyone in-between was talking about God and conviction and presence and knowability. I took it all in, all of these other stories, these voices not my own telling of a God I no longer knew in the way I had once known God.

Francis.

Francis and his prayer that in the doing of faithful things, we are one with Christ.

I could not hold that then.

I can barely hold it now.

That semester, I sit in on Dr. Candler's graduate-level class in Christology. *Sitting in* means I keep up with the readings but I don't really have to do anything else. The course explores an extension of what Dr. Candler had first introduced us to in Twentieth Century: the question of Jesus, what it means to say that God is fully God and fully Man.

Our readings are Scripture, deuterocanonicals, early church writers, medievals, reformers, moderns. We trace through time the way the church has wrestled with the impossible confession that God should die and God should live, that God should have flesh and yet be spirit, that God would come at all to redeem us, that

God would call hallowed and holy bodies that sag and age and die before they are renewed to rise again.

In the Incarnation, God comes so close to us. He draws near.

Later, Antonia would tell me about yoga as a way of thinking about that nearness, about how *namaste* means, roughly, "I bow to you." In the Incarnation, Jesus bows to us. Breathe in and hold the breath. Hold it for a moment. Hold that meditation: Jesus bows to us. In taking on our flesh, in becoming the God who is with us, God is bowing to us. God is humbling Godself to be as we are. God honors us so that we may have the means to fully honor God.

In the silence I wonder about the nearness and find it an offense.

I don't want a God who is that close.

A God who is that close is too much to hold.

And yet.

Every Sunday, every Wednesday, in the large sanctuary or in the side chapel of St. Paul's, I confess that God is held.

There is a prayer of Saint Francis that marvels after this Jesus who hides himself beneath a wafer and in wine.[38] In the days of Silence I am not sure still what I believe about the Eucharist, but I know that I am clinging to any sign that he is near, and so Communion becomes as much a prayer in and of itself than any bow or dip or crossing of myself.

"Be near," I am pleading, when I receive that bread and that wine. "Come back."

Antonia is now always beside me at that rail, and she knows the prayer I am praying. We have been going to St. Paul's together for months, and she is careful to ask about the silence only when I am ready to say something about it, which is rare. But she is beside me, and that is, itself, a sort of gift that is hard to ever fully see, except that if Jesus took us on, made bodies hallowed, then it is possible to look over at the Communion rail when you feel that he is gone and to see him there kneeling beside you in the person of a close friend.

And that keeps you going.

That keeps you held.

It has to.

Antonia and I spend a lot of time together at Common Grounds.

We talk about class, about Faith, about whether or not we'll catch sight of Jerry between teaching, cycling, and going to classes at the seminary. More often than not we end up seeing him, and the three of us catch up quickly before he runs off to something else. He is doing well, in spite of things, and we watch him carefully for signs that we need to intervene.

The conversations between Antonia and me are hard to explain. They are always half. One of us is reading something and says to the other, "I'm thinking about saints and intercession—"

And the other sees what's being read and jumps in thirteen or more sentences ahead in the conversation. It's the way of us, a language all our own. We were the only two students we knew from Baylor who were going to St. Paul's, who didn't want to be Roman Catholic but also didn't have a problem with it. We were asking the same questions, pressing toward the same wonderings about the nearness and otherness of God in the ordinary and in our daily lives. Antonia had grown up with charismatics, so her entire perspective on invoking the Holy Spirit over anything was shaded dramatically, while I was just trying to make sense of why I was comfortable crossing myself and why the action in and of itself felt like prayer.

So we sorted each other, held the ideas and the questions for one another, recommended reading and perspective and this one song or this one poem or this one thing that was said that one time in this one way as something of a piece of the puzzle to hold together the larger, moving ideas that rolled in like thunderstorms in our hearts.

"Hilary is a really good writer," she says, tactlessly, within minutes of me telling her that Addison and I have broken up.

"She is."

"She is." And she went back to her book.

On Saturday mornings, Sam comes over to my room with his Bible and journal. We sit together and read the lectionary texts and pray; we talk about God; we talk about the feeling of loss; and eventually we circle to hopefulness, though it is fleeting for me.

A few weeks in, he starts bringing his guitar as well.

He is skilled musically in ways that echo in me, the way he plays puts me in a place of peace. He sits in my room and plays nothing or plays everything, slowly and worshipfully, and those days are the days that I feel like I can remember again why we do all of it, why we read Scripture and why we pray and why we say in Communion Christ is made known.

There is healing in those plucked strings, careful and slow.

He has stopped asking about Hilary, which is kind. He is tired of my lying. I am tired of lying to him. We both plan to apply to St. Andrews. He for Scripture and Theology, I for the arts. We imagine it will be nice if it happens.

I am quietly certain it will not.

"It doesn't really make sense, I know, but I think I'm only supposed to apply to St. Andrews."

I told Jeffrey this in early November, just before Advent, on a breezy Wednesday morning with a storm rolling in. He asked me how I knew and I shrugged.

"I woke up with peace. I guess. I woke up with something, at least."

He knew about the Silence, about the feeling of absence. I had told him earlier, around the time it happened, and his eyes moved over my face looking for a sign of whether or not this was the end of it.

"No." I replied to the unasked question. "God's still gone. This is just ... a crumb I suppose."

"Right." He nodded. "*Lek-leka.*"

Lek-leka. לֶךְ־לְךָ

It is what God speaks to Abraham in Genesis 12. It means, *Go.* The whole verse, or at least the part that Jeffrey wanted me to pay attention to, is "Go and I will show you."

God will show where.

You don't always get to know when you set out on the journey. In fact, Abraham will wander in a circle before he is sent out to where he is eventually to be.

Applying only to St. Andrews was that, I suppose, a going with the belief that God would show me. But God also wasn't much around anymore, so it felt a silly game of chance. But I went. I supposed it was counted to me as righteousness.

One can hope.

I counted the other morning, and it's ninety-seven.

I bought ninety-seven books in the Silence.

They filled my shelves and littered my floor. Saints and commentary writers and prayer books.

I told you at one point I stopped reading them.

Did I tell you that at one point I stopped believing them too?
I don't know when. It was so quiet, I didn't know myself.

The action of grace in our hearts is secret and silent.
Weil.
I turn it over and over and over.
It clings to me.
Maybe one day I will understand.
Or not.
Maybe that's the point.

I have already written about Christmas. I have already told you about Sam keeping vigil for me on Christmas Eve when we sang the song about Jesus being near and he wasn't.

But it's important for me to say it again.

It is important for me to retell that thing and then tell it for what it was: I didn't want to see it. I didn't want him to be that near. The Jesus of the nativity is a loud, crying baby covered in afterbirth. He is crude and unrefined. He is too human, too near, too apparently broken.

Like me.

He is too much like me.

And I am not enough like him.

January 2012.

(Have you noticed? I stopped naming the seasons. I didn't in those days. It was easier.)

I take up painting when I can't even bring myself to repeat the written prayers. On the floor of my dorm room, I work out abstract forms, abstract prayers, pour out myself onto the canvas and name them spiritual things to try to feel the spiritual within me. They are called "Annunciation" and "Book of Common Prayer" and "Genesis 1:1/John 1:1." They are beautiful, though languid, signs that I am a novice in this practice and still don't know what I want it to be. But it is perhaps the newness that roots me, though I am not aware at the time the root has held. The newness makes me slip away from the comfort of the normal, makes me forget that God feels absent, and in that I discover in the Silence there is still something to be done.

The painting is prayer. The prayer is in the doing.

In the beginning was the deed.

No.

In the beginning was the Word. Visceral, painful, present, and still present now, a painting on a wall speaks long after the last brushstroke. It is a sort of everlasting prayer. It is there for the days you can't pray or won't or wouldn't know where to begin. I discover that later, much later, but when I do, I can see the paintings for what they were and I can say, "There is God. And there. And there."

It was on an afternoon when I was painting on my floor that Hilary and I Skyped again.

I had been reading her blog every day because her words were breath when I had forgotten how to breathe. She was fullness and tenderness, like the paintings a kind of prayer, and to touch her words was to touch God again, even if it lingered only for a moment. I am thinking this when she tells me she might give it all up, that she doesn't see the point of writing in that space where no one seems to be reading.

I want to tell her I do. I want to tell her that I do because I love her, but I hold it back because the question of brokenness and fullness and pouring out still circles and encircles me.

"Please don't."

I manage that. I manage to at least say that.

Then I have an idea, a small idea that drifts across my mind and heart.

"What if we wrote letters to each other? You always seem to write better when you have someone to respond to, a prompt to respond to, so why don't you just write a letter to me on your blog, and then I'll write back to you on mine, and we'll go back and forth."

She looked at me so kindly my heart swelled against my rib-cage and I couldn't breathe.

"Okay."

"Okay."

This is how God returns.

Quietly.

But in a way that bursts the smallness of your heart.

Ten

———— ◆ ————

TABLES

As usual, God catches me by surprise.

Much later, after Baylor, I'm unpacking, slowly pulling out the icons of another life, trying to relocate myself in my parent's home, in my old room, with my old high school self. The self of surety, of contentment in being in the circle of the faithful who are the ones who know.

There's a box I've kept of cards and letters I wanted to hold on to before Baylor that I'm sorting, combining with the box I started my freshman year and built up over the time away. I find a birthday card my mother gave me the year before, a few weeks before Jesus packed up the boxes and left.

The card is weighty, and I wonder, halfhearted and nearly bankrupt, if I had passed over a gift card. Inside is a small, ugly little cross magnet. I would never use it. I would never buy it. It repulses me with its commonness and pointlessness.

What sort of thing do you put under a cross magnet?

Who makes the cross a magnet to begin with?

And I think this, I keep thinking this, as I find myself reading the word in script typeface across the beam of the cross, where his arms were stretched out so wide the whole of the creation was held within them: *Trust.*

Boldfaced.

Trust.

Before. Near the end of Epiphany 2012.

Sam hears from St. Andrews quickly with an acceptance. He bangs on my door early one morning and excitedly tells me about his offer while I try to hide how certain this makes me that I have not gotten in. I congratulate him. I tell him he deserves it and that I am proud.

But I am also jealous. I am jealous that he knows what his next step is when I don't know mine. I am angry at the silent God who maybe doesn't much care anymore what does or does not happen to me. I start to wonder if I should have applied elsewhere, if this was just like The Well all over again, if it was foolhardy and pathetic and a desperate attempt to make my life seem more exciting than it actually was.

I sat in Jeffrey's office often the next few weeks, Tommye Lou's too. I would tell them how maybe it was all just a big farce, that my faith was a kind of exercise in false humility, that I had fooled myself long enough to ignore that I really didn't believe, really didn't trust, and I was just trying to make it up as I went along.

"Preston, the greatest gift you have is your ability to abide in God's presence."

Tommye Lou speaks it slowly after I have puddled the uncertainty before her for twenty minutes.

"But right now you keep wanting God to come to you on your own terms. God is present. Right now. Right here. Maybe God's just answering a different question."

I start joking about giving up on graduate school, moving to

Connecticut, getting married, and writing books for the rest of my life.

"So there's a girl?" Tommye Lou arches an eyebrow.

"No." I say hastily. "No, just. It's an idea."

"I see."

She nods. She knows, but she's polite enough to not press the point.

As part of the final course in our Great Texts major, Antonia and I, along with Caroline and Maddee, who had been in and out of classes with us since our freshman year, took the Capstone module under Phillip Donnelley. Capstone was designed as the sequencing course, the reflective survey of texts already visited now reintroduced to ask a larger question of the Western corpus as a whole. Essentially, How then shall we live?

The four of us convened with a few others around the boardroom table we had grown to love and reworked our way through Aristotle, Shakespeare, Plato, Shelley, Milton, Huxley, and Swift. There was a small coup over the absence of saints on the reading list, Milton all but barely passing the scrutiny we placed on the need for devotional literature to be part of the final experience in our major of books. When scheduling meant we would forgo a play of Shakespeare, we strongly requested additional class days so that we could still discuss it. We were completely and totally in love with the nature of that program, with the opportunity to marvel and wonder at the words that had been handed down to us by those gone before. Great Texts taught you to love the tradition, not just the Christian tradition but the tradition that was the ideas and ponderings and hopes and failings of generations long past.

Perhaps the most significant thing we were given in that last class, as obvious as it may seem, was the question "What kind of book is this?" Dr. Donnelly patiently reminded us that when we begin to discuss big, sweeping ideas, we have a tendency to gather up all the words as the same, to place all the wonderings into the same space, without care for the importance of genre, of purposed form. So in the end, saints snuck in there.

Antonia and I left that particular class thinking about the Bible, about how we are guilty, often, of doing the same thing. We take Genesis and Luke, like DLJ had mentioned, and put them together without first asking the question "What sort of book is Genesis?" and "What sort of book is Luke?" How we answer is important, because if Genesis is not trying to tell the same kind of story that Luke is trying to tell, then how we interpret and live out and into those stories changes.

"It's too big to do on our own," Antonia said as we were crossing the street to Common Grounds. "The Bible, God, it's too much to try to do on our own. It's too much to pretend we know well enough in the first place. We need the conversation, the big table where everyone comes together, where we ask, 'What kind of book is this?' or 'What is the character of God?' or 'What is the Eucharist?' and then we need to listen. We need to breathe in the old and current and the possibility of the new."

"We have the weirdest conversations," I said, as a point of benediction.

"All the things," she agreed, and we made the sign of the cross to the statue of Francis as we walked past.

Jerry ended up leaving the seminary, which was for the best. He settled into an apartment in Waco and he, Antonia, and I resumed a version of Fire Circle Wine Nights. He was working on new stories, taking a break from his longer work for a time. The darkness that had swept in the previous semester was not gone, but the presence of it was now part of our common vernacular. Speaking of it returned the power to him and then the power to us in our circle of friendship and companionship. He was dating a woman who was above all things joyful, and she pressed that joy against his sorrow, and I think in more ways than one helped him stand upright again.

"I may marry her," he says one night, when we are doing dishes together.

"You will," I smile, taking a glass from him and running a tea towel along the inside. "Are you happy?"

"I am."

"Good."

"Are you?"

I bite my lower lip. "I am ..." I trail off and sigh. "I am sure that I am supposed to be."

He looks away from me, rinses a plate, and then hands it back my way.

"You haven't talked about stillness in a while."

It is an unexpected turn.

"I guess I haven't."

He nods, rinses another plate, hands it back again.

We do the rest of the dishes in silence.

In late Epiphany, Grant and I, and often Antonia, go to midweek Eucharist together in the side chapel of St. Paul's. There's never more than twenty or so of us, often fewer, and we say a truncated form of the prayers of the people and then partake in Communion. Father Chuck or Mother Judy—she is new and I like her, because she reminds me of my grandmothers—offers the Bread and Wine and whispers over our heads that they are given to keep us in everlasting life.

Afterward, Grant and I drive back to campus, and he parks outside of my dorm. We have a habit now, talking for an hour or more one on one, decompressing the world and our longings with one another. He is so fiercely good, and it surprises me each time I encounter it. He is wondering about important things, like whether the deaf community feels like it has a full place in the church or if he should become a priest or an academic or some variation on both. He asks questions, true questions, and there is something that happens in that car and in those words that I do not understand until much later. I am entrusted with something rare, asked to hold the gift of him, the weight of what he longs for and seeks, and I realize that the only way to hold such a thing is if you are yourself able to be filled, able to hold.

Like the Body and Blood, it seems too much, but you find that God makes room in you.

I was accepted to St. Andrews early on a Tuesday morning.

I told Sam first, then my parents, and then walked across campus in sweatpants and T-shirt to tell Dr. Jeffrey.

"Are you surprised?"

"Yes!" I replied, somewhat indignant.

"I just was thinking that this may be a sign of having heard well." He smiled, softly, the pastoral way.

"Blessings on you, lad. Go write me a thesis chapter."

This too is how God returns.

Slowly.

So slow that you don't realize God hasn't really left until much later, when you realize you hadn't really left either.

Ash Wednesday.

It was after the reading from Isaiah, during the Second Epistle to the Corinthians. He appeared to be homeless, clothes hanging off his frame, walking down the center aisle of the nave of St. Paul's, and I wondered if he wouldn't stop until he reached the altar, because his steps seemed so determined. He took a seat near the front. He stood with us during the reading of the Gospel, he did not cross himself with us when the homily began. He raised his hand once, during the homily, and Father Chuck gently looked from him. This was right, for a kind, older woman was already on her way to sit beside this stranger, to pat his shoulder, to lean in and listen to him whisper into her ear.

I couldn't stop wondering if he was hungry.

We were five minutes into the homily and my insides were churning. I couldn't stop looking at the man and wondering if he needed to be fed, how he would be fed. There wasn't a lunch after the service, there wasn't necessarily going to be food to be found. Then I was thinking about the sandwich shop, the one on the corner several blocks away that I had never been inside but had passed often.

I sat and debated the inner voice in me, because I have not heard God in so long, I could not be sure if it was Voice or voice, God or self. Things were lost in the translation.

Today, if you would hear his voice, do not harden your hearts.

What was I thinking?

If it sounds like Jesus.

It was the middle of the homily. I left my copy of the prayer book, the leather-bound one I love, slid past Sam and Antonia, and kept my eyes down and away from these stained-glass saints as I walked to the back of the nave, breath coming short.

The sun was pushing hard out from the clouds, and I wished I had my sunglasses. It was several city blocks to the sandwich shop, and at one point I found myself lost. I was turning over too much in my mind about what this man would want. If I were hungry, what sort of deli slice would I value, what would be extra special, would be a gift?

I crossed against two lights and entered the shop. There was a line, which frustrated me. If this was right, shouldn't it be easier, a path made clear? I considered asking the people in front if I could go ahead of them, for I was about my Father's business, but I still wasn't even sure that I was.

What if the man wasn't hungry at all? What if this was not going to be gift but offense?

So I waited in line, still debating, still wondering, and at one point I noticed on the menu board a sandwich like the one I had thought of, with the addition of mayonnaise. I considered, however foolishly, that it might just be Providence if that man should also like mayonnaise.

I walked briskly back to the church, knowing by this point I had missed the imposition of the ashes. My heart was pounding violently in my chest, aching to be set free. I gripped the sandwich tight as I waited for a light to turn and the traffic to stop and, in the anger of my exhaustion, hurled a prayer like a javelin into the heavens and demanded to know why this silence of God had been so palpable lately, why this absurd act of buying a sandwich for someone who might not even need it was the closest to God's touch I had felt in months.

And God replied as the red hand on the sign telling me to stay turned to the white stick figure telling me to walk. I heard him by the words I had read the night before in *Father Elijah*: "I ask only that you walk neither behind nor before, to the left or the right, but that you walk in the midst, even into the valley of the shadow."[39]

And I wept. I wept at the corner of North Sixth Street and Columbus Avenue, holding a sandwich, no ashes on my forehead, but ashes pressed hard into the flesh of my heart.

For God is good, even in the shadow of joy, even on this side of God's Silence.

I sat outside the nave while the service finished, looking up the prayer book on my iPhone and following along. When the doors opened, when the people shuffled out in silence, ashen foreheads and bowed heads, I quietly made my way to the woman sitting with the man and passed the sandwich to her. She would know if it would be gift or offense to him, she would know what to do.

"I thought he might be hungry."

Because I was hungry. Because the most I could muster right then was reaching out and passing off what I hoped was blessing, because the ashes of my collected self could only manage that.

Hilary and I write a letter on our blogs to each other every Tuesday and Thursday.

I forget one week and she patiently reminds me that I have.

(I forget because I am trying to distance myself, to keep myself from having to confess how much I fall for her every time I read something she writes, how when she speaks of God I feel like God is near again, how I would give up everything to be with her and knowing that, particularly, terrifies me.)

She comes through Texas once, only for a day, which coincides with an event that I can't get out of. For six hours I walk back and forth from the parking lot thinking I'll just get in my car and go, blow the event off, and finally meet her, kiss her, tell her that I have loved her for so long.

But I don't.

Jerry and Antonia come with me to my house for Easter Break. We spend the weekend attending a variety of churches: Baptist, Episcopal, and Anglican. We talk about faith, the rooted parts of the faith, the daily and breathed and honest parts. When we go to Easter Vigil, we witness the baptism of a newborn, and Antonia and I marvel at the meaning of it, that from birth the child has been told she is to be grafted into the family of God. On the drive back in the dark, we both somewhat exclaim, "I'm sort of okay with infant baptism now."

Jerry from the backseat laughs. He's Presbyterian; he's been all right with infant baptism for a long time.

Antonia and I still go back and forth on it. We message each other or call and put up the arguments and raise the questions, put the voices in the room, and wonder after the answers. What that night marked was nothing less than a simple and profound willingness to hear in ways I myself had resisted before: theology is contextual, it is breathed, it is lived, and if it is not understood in the everyday habit of being, of habituated prayer, there is no point.

On Easter we went to HopePointe, which was bright and luminous and full of life. We took Communion together at the same rail, the rail at the Table of the Lord, where we must all come, in and across time, and do come, in our own ways, to be a part of the great conversation of the faith.

I have never before felt something in Communion, in a proud sense. Perhaps the wafer sticking to the roof of my mouth was something, but that is as close as I have come. Most of the time I feel nothing but quiet. Quiet. Because I am learning that my place at that Table is a still one, an abiding one, a welcoming one.

The Silence is not a punishment, it's the gift of learning how to hear more fully.

God in others, God in the midst of the everyday, God, without pretense, in the ordinary chaos of a beautiful world.

Eastertide.

On a warm May day, I crossed campus toward Jeffrey's office for the last time as an undergraduate. I had emailed him, well before my thesis defense, about wanting to talk baptism and the

Eucharist. I had questions, certain uncertainties, and an intuited knowing that he would give me the answers that I needed, or at least the confidence to frame the questions appropriately.

He asked how I was. I said I was fine, that I had come to a place of peace. To this he nodded curtly, twinkle in eye, reading me better than I read myself. I waded through a muddled reflection on baptism, then stumbled my way into Eucharist.

"I believe in the Real Presence," I said simply, "but I have no idea what that means."

It was a silly thing to say, perhaps. How do you believe what you do not understand, though I think there's something of Saint Paul's reasoning in that. But what I meant was that I had always taken the phrasing *Real Presence* to sound as true as anything else I had heard or read concerning the Eucharist. What that meant I wasn't entirely clear on, what that meant I had spent the past three years trying to understand.

Jeffrey nodded again.

"It's like a drama, Preston. Take a staging of *Oedipus*, for instance. The actor playing Oedipus is standing off stage and someone in the cast announces, 'Here comes Oedipus!' and the actor comes out on stage. Is the actor really, in the sense of literally, Oedipus? No. But do we grant, do we believe, do we for the sake of what is unfolding say that in this moment, this actor is unto us Oedipus? We do. In this sense, we say that Oedipus is present to us, is really present."

The line from Rite I clung to me: *and be unto us His body and His blood.*

Something from Handle's *Messiah*: *unto us a Child is given.*

I walked back across campus to my dorm, singing "Great and Marvelous" very softly, the sun, like the elevated Host, like the Real Presence, shining bright overhead, a visual metaphor from O'Connor's short story, aptly titled, "A Temple of the Holy Ghost."

⋈

Notice, a sort of return: spontaneous singing.

The Psalmist: *Dwell in the land and cultivate faithfulness.*

There is a lot of dwelling in this interim space. Dwelling and waiting are different things. To dwell is to believe that you are rooted for a time, perhaps a long time, and you create routine and method in this space. To wait is simply to anticipate, there is no need for routine or even method, except to distract.

I am being pulled into the place of dwelling; in the rhythm of the church year and the cycles of the daily offices, I am to dwell.

Notice: it is in the space of dwelling that the song comes.

The last time Barbara clasps my hands, she tells me a story that I have heard more than once from her, but now hear fully for the first time. She tells me that after her husband walked away from the faith for a time, she spent ten years praying only one prayer: *Lord, keep me safe.* From that prayer she went to Asia and to Europe, sought God on the mountains and in the plains, in monasteries and churches, and traveled the world in search of the elusive Presence of the Lord. Eventually, she and her husband settled in Waco, and after throwing open the phonebook and throwing down her finger, she ended up at St. Paul's. She went one Sunday and never went anywhere else again. Her husband joined her there two years later and lived happily serving the Lord until he died a decade or so after that.

"See," she said tenderly, "if I could give you anything to take with you on your journey from here, it would be this: Pray that God would keep you safe, then go search everywhere until you find him. You'd be surprised where he'll take you. I think you'll find you're already a bit surprised by where you've been."

I would be at my kitchen table in St. Andrews, reading Madeleine L'Engle nearly a year later when I would get a text from Antonia letting me know that Barbara had died.

What is the line from the liturgy?

Departed this life in Thy faith and fear.

We graduated on a Saturday.

Caroline, Maddee, Antonia, and I met at Common Grounds that morning, ordered coffees in our finery, and drove over to the stadium to put on our trash bags — how we with little affection referred to our graduation gowns — and joined the thousands of others milling about trying to figure out where they were supposed to be. It was odd, the moment we looked at each other, realizing only four of us were walking in our ridiculous major of books and ideas, and we were numbered among thousands of others who had majored in concrete things like business and math.

I remember our hands reaching across one another and clasping. I remember walking across the stage and the multitude of embraces. Off the stage, I remember when our professors lined up to congratulate us, to hug us, to tell us we were some of their favorites. And I remember feeling that it was the most ordinary of days, how nothing much had really happened, except a life had been lived on these grounds and now it was time to uproot, to plant somewhere else, our trash bags billowing like clergy robes as we walked.

That night, Sam and I helped pack Grant's apartment.

I brought wine and champagne because it is the sort of thing you do in those moments. I was there before Sam, and Grant and I spent time talking about idle things, about Scotland and graduate work. He talked to me about his future, his doubts, and in his own way, in that way that breaks me to think of because it is that certain kind of beautiful, his love.

When Sam arrived, we drank out of the bottle, the label of which read *Franciscan*, because, of course, I needed Francis around, even as icon in wine bottle form, for the impossible feat of leaving these two brothers I loved.

We spent the evening talking about ordinary things.

There were bills to be paid, something read in *The New Yorker*, a question about logistics for Sam and Chérie's wedding. (The engagement was still pending, but soon.) Eventually, these were exhausted, each word, and we were left in the last hour opening the champagne and making toasts, one after another, toward the other two and toward the companionship we had built.

We toasted the gift of God, and because it was still Eastertide, we toasted our Christ.

"Christ is risen," I saluted.

"He is risen indeed," they responded.

Glasses clinked. Perching on a corner of the couch between the boxes, I tore out a small piece of my heart and buried it there between them to await its own resurrection, its own certain hope in the restoration of all things, in the end of every good-bye ever spoken.

The next morning, my family and Antonia's gathered at St. Paul's. Aside from the extraordinary circumstance of our families joining us at church, it was a relatively uneventful service. I don't remember what Father Chuck shared, and I barely recall going forward to receive the Eucharist one last time from the hands of such a gracious priest.

I remember the awkwardness, a perfect close to my time in that church, when Antonia and I went forward to receive a blessing on our graduation. I had emailed Father Chuck the day before asking if it was all right, and, when it came time to bless birthdays and anniversaries, I was nervous and wondered if he had forgotten, so I told Antonia we should go ahead and go up. We should have waited. He was going to call us up after, but there we were, with the anniversary couples, as awkward as we had been in our own ways the first Sundays we stumbled down that center aisle.

I remember now only colors, only the way the sun spilled through the stained glass, only how bright and iridescent the congregation was, a temple of the Holy Ghost, a people of God, a family that had unknowingly taken me in and given me words when I could not find them to pray.

I left Waco that evening, the prayers of this people, this particular people, journeying me onward.

I would be confirmed an Anglican a year later.

I would still have my questions about baptism, and I would find it odd at times to be a liberal in the midst of conservatives, but it would be the fulfillment of what Father Chuck had spoken over me, that confirmation is saying that you are willing to take not only the good from them but also the bad.

HopePointe, its wash of charismatic flare and rootedness in the tradition, was an outward manifestation of my own soul. You never know exactly what's hanging around, what scrap from one saint or what maybe-sort-of prophetic word. My parents would be there, by my side, and they would take Communion with me too.

In that action they would affirm a simple and yet beautiful thing: you are not being handed over from us, we are all at the same Table of the same Lord.

Sam and I will spend another year together in Scotland before we have to geographically part ways. He and Chérie will be married that December, and the three of us will enjoy a handful of months in the same place before they move to Belgium so that Sam can begin an advanced masters and PhD in early church studies.

I will return to finish my masters in America and to work at HopePointe for a year as the assistant to a bishop and as a teacher for a new catechism curriculum that is being piloted the same year I arrive.

I will live close enough to Grant, who will be a teacher in Houston, to see him nearly every weekend.

Antonia will spend a year in Waco and then begin a masters of divinity at Duke, calling me every other day to debate whether or not she should be ordained.

Jerry will start his MBA at Baylor and will get married the following year in May.

Sam will be the best man at my wedding the following June, and Chérie a bridesmaid. Grant will be a groomsman, Antonia a bridesmaid, and Jerry will be there in spirit, still on his honeymoon.

There will be a moment between Sam and me, in the middle of a Scottish wood, in which I will tell him that I have spent too much of my life being certain about God, and I am just feeling free enough again to wonder.

He will laugh and shake his head.

"You've been doing that already for a long time now. You just need to start writing it down to see it."

I will stop, open my mouth, close it, then open it again.

"Yes. I guess I do."

The form pride takes can be surprising. The Church of No Windows prided itself on everything it wasn't, while I prided myself on everything I thought I was.

For a long time after I first began attending St. Paul's, I carried the word *Eucharist* around like it was a weapon. Anytime I was with anyone, I saw fit to forgo other words like *Communion* or *Lord's Supper* in favor of the "right" word for the event. Even if the other person had used *Communion* the entire time they spoke, I insisted on calling it the *Eucharist* in a kind of pointed, knowing way.

Worse, I did this mostly with my parents. I carried around *Eucharist* like I was harpooning it into the word *evangelical*, tactlessly deploying usage whenever possible, from planning my attendance at church Sunday mornings to the general, dropped reference in ordinary conversations about building a porch in our backyard the following summer.

In Paul's First Letter to the Corinthians, the same book I had scrawled the word *Eucharist* beside instructions about Communion my first year at St. Paul's, the actual Saint Paul writes, "What do you have that you did not receive? And if you did receive it, why do you boast as if you had not received it?"

I had missed the point of the Eucharist entirely by obsessing over how to name it. There's nothing more zealous than a convert— Paul is a good case study to go by—and in my joy of finding a place I had fit, I stumbled around trying to make everyone else fit there too. But the message of the Lord's Supper, Communion, Eucharist, transcends all that.

If we get tripped up by the words about God, we miss God in the process. It took me a long time, but I eventually gave up the need always to call the Eucharist the Eucharist and instead use the words Communion, Lord's Supper, and Eucharist with an interchangeable grace. I let circumstance dictate my word choice. I let context determine my response. Because there was a time there where I and The Church of No Windows were essentially one and the same. We were both fighting, clawing, thrashing to prove who we were not.

But grace comes into the cracked places, and one day I said Communion and meant it, profoundly, as much as I would have meant Eucharist. It was about that time I became comfortable again with the word *evangelical* too.

⋈

Hilary.

The fullness of that story is perhaps for another time, but it would take a year for the two of us actually to see one another. But once we do, we will move quickly. We will know that we have been in love for two years, that we had fallen for each other the first time we had read each other's words, and we will be engaged within a handful of months.

We will be impossibly happy.

We will marvel that it took us so long to figure it out.

"But we did," she will tell me that night along the waterway.

"But we did," I will repeat.

Eventually, I bought the statue of Saint Francis from Common Grounds.

Blake, the current owner, very generously accepted my offer of payment after I spent six months trying to broker a deal. The statue was original to the store itself, so to remove it was to take a piece of its history with me, not just the history that I had with it. But after that many cappuccinos and the hours I spent there, writing pages that would eventually become this book, Blake let me part with my patron saint in peace.

As I carried Francis to my car, I thought about a stray comment Blake had made as I left, about how he would always catch snippets of the conversation Antonia and I or Jerry and I or someone else and I would be having, how they would always be so interesting, so engaging, how those conversations wove God in and out of everyday things effortlessly. I thought about sacred space, about how in high church tradition, we believe that space can be consecrated and made holy slowly, over time, by the prayers that are pressed into that space. I wondered about all those conversations, about all the times we spoke life, about meeting Sam and talking with Antonia about Hilary and Crina, from early in the year of Silence, asking if we were going to be all right.

In the end we were.

I thought about the verse that says God's word does not return void.

As I placed Francis in the backseat of my car to drive him home, I considered that maybe this had something to do with the fullness of that word's return.

"And what about now? Do you hear God speak now?"

This happens before.

Erin and I meet for coffee close to the end of my senior year at Baylor. Erin is an extraordinarily talented painter who attends a nondenominational, sometimes charismatic church, and at the same time reads the medieval mystic Julian of Norwich. We sat on the big red couch in Common Grounds and shared the fragmented pieces of ourselves. I told her about Jesus and the silence of God.

That's when she asks me.

"Yes," I finally say, tentatively. "But it's different."

I shift, draw my legs up to myself.

"I'm learning to hear by other people. I'm learning to hear in the small and quiet things." My words fumble, falter; I try to make the theological abstractions of my situation stay in the abstract, in the irresponsible, but it comes crashing back into me and I blurt out the story about Ash Wednesday that year.

I tell it as if I am hearing it myself for the first time.

"You don't have the ashes inscribed on your forehead that Ash Wednesday, but you have them inscribed on your heart. Because God makes tables in the wilderness. God makes them everywhere if we'd only learn to look."

And we both have tears in our eyes, and we both make no apology for them.

I'm thinking about Eileen again.

I'm thinking about Eileen and the kaleidoscope.

What I hadn't quite understood at first, when it felt that Jesus had packed up the boxes, was that while the image of God I was seeing had changed, the pieces that portrayed the image hadn't. For nearly two decades, the Holy Spirit had been bringing in pieces of a theological imagination.

On that day in September, sitting on that couch, he shifted the wheel.

All the pieces — the colors, the shapes, the raw materials — remained the same. The vision was new. The way of seeing was new. The way of hearing was new. God remained the same.

He gets you there.

"And what about now? Do you hear God speak now?"

I keep coming back to that question.

Again, this happens before. Eastertide 2012.

Antonia and I sit in Common Grounds on the last day of classes, two weeks before we graduate from our undergraduate degree in books. We only half talk to each other, doing our best actually to accomplish something other than chatter, a looming final paper due the next week that we pretend to work on, when all the while what we're really doing is eavesdropping on the first date unfolding in front of us and, twenty minutes later, the flock of graduate student TAs who come in to grade papers and complain about the inability of the junior in college to construct a thesis statement, and who speak to each other as if they were being graded on their ability to utter the word *epistemological* with the same practiced casualness as I use to order my coffee.

Eventually, the lack of work being done is obvious and we break down and talk. We circle over our favorite parts of books and think through the hurtles of the oral defense we have in three days, when all those books in our major of books are supposed to be recalled and articulated into a seamless whole. We talk about postmodernism and how we can't stand to read Hobbes. Antonia talks about arranging books according to who needs to be talking to whom, dead or alive, and how Martin Luther and Saint Teresa have been locked in wordless proximity for the whole semester.

Because our conversations turn this way, we talk about the Eucharist in the twelfth century, about Real Presence, about grace, and then about the timeliness of God. This invariably gets us talking about how we came into Baylor determined that we were secure in not only our Faith but also denominational allegiances—me the Southern Baptist and she the confused-free-church-somewhat-charismatic. We appropriately juxtapose this thought process with wondering what day the bishop is coming to bless those being confirmed at St. Paul's and thinking through how our families will fare when they come to church with us on Mother's Day, the day after our graduation, which happens liturgically to be the last Sunday in Eastertide before the Ascension of Christ.

"It's weird," Antonia says. "The process to here has been so tenuous. I can see all the places where it could have gone differently. They're just lily pads along the way. That's what Anne Lamott calls them."

We talk about free will then, about how we have it but God has it, about how we're here because God brought us here even though we chose, and that hedge of protection that flies around evangelical prayers the way *give us Thy peace* does in the Episcopal comes to my mind.

I think about it on the way back to my dorm, on my way upstairs. I think about how I am grateful that God has set me on this path, has been my hedge of protection, has let me read this saint and that one, has given me the lens God has given me. But then I realize that there's something outside of my choices in it and God guiding of me. For there were professors and authors and friends and parents and mail carriers who had been uniquely formed, in no small part, to get me here. And they had their people getting them here too. And I keep tracing it back like a huge genealogy of the human race, back and further back to creation myth and Adam and Eve, then further still, to that time before there was time, before the foundations of the world, where God foreknew it all and decided, in wild mercy, to invite us all into the narrative God was going to unfold.

These tables. These tables of abundant and ordinary mercies that all point back to the one Table, the place where we say we meet God, where God is made known.

Yes, the whole process from start to finish is tenuous.

I am thinking about the lily pads.

We're leaping from instability to instability like we have a choice in our landing, which we do, in part, but we forget that spatial positioning is more than just left or right or across, leaping this way and that.

It's up and down too. It's trusting that the lily pad we land on will keep afloat.

And in the end, it's the Water that keeps holding us up.

SUGGESTED READING

Several people have noted that since books were such an important part of my journey—and still are—it would be good for me to include a selection that I would recommend as particularly significant. Below, I have chosen five books for each chapter that reflect what I was reading during the events the chapter covers. I suppose they function as expanded endnotes, or that "gloss" Marie de France spoke of.

One — SILENCE

The Book of Common Prayer: 1979. The Episcopal Church. Oxford: Oxford University Press, 2008.

Webber, Christopher L. *Give Us Grace: An Anthology of Anglican Prayers.* New York: Morehouse, 2004.

Schnackenberg, Gjertrud. *Supernatural Love: Poems 1976–1992.* New York: Farrar, Straus and Giroux, 2000.

Némirovsky, Irène. *Fire in the Blood.* New York: Vintage, 2007.

Winner, Lauren. *Still: Notes on a Mid-Faith Crisis.* San Francisco: HarperOne, 2012.

Two — BEGINNINGS

Ishiguro, Kazuo. *Never Let Me Go.* New York: Vintage, 2005.

Capote, Truman. *Breakfast at Tiffany's.* New York: Penguin Classics, 2000.

Kingsolver, Barbara. *The Poisonwood Bible.* New York: HarperCollins, 1998.

Wharton, Edith. *The House of Mirth.* New York: Barnes & Noble Classics, 2004.

Atwood, Margaret. *The Handmaid's Tale*. New York: Anchor, 1986.

Three — CERTAINTY

Foster, Richard. *Celebration of Discipline*. San Francisco: HarperOne, 1998.

Maguire, Gregory. *Wicked: The Life and Times of the Wicked Witch of the West*. New York: HarperCollins, 1995.

Wheatley, Phillis. *Complete Writings*. New York: Penguin Classics, 2001.

Willard, Dallas. *The Divine Conspiracy: Rediscovering Our Hidden Life in God*. San Francisco: HarperOne, 1998.

Anselm. *The Prayers and Meditations of Saint Anselm with the Proslogion*. New York: Penguin Classics, 1986.

Four — FRACTURES

Marie de France. *The Lais of Marie de France*. New York: Penguin, 1999.

Boethius. *The Consolation of Philosophy*. New York: Penguin, 2000.

Dante. *Paradiso*. New York: Modern Library, 2007.

Wright, N. T. *Surprised by Hope: Rethinking Heaven, the Resurrection, and the Mission of the Church*. San Francisco: HarperOne, 2008.

Robinson, Marilynne. *Gilead: A Novel*. New York: Picador, 2006.

Five — DESERT

Ordway, Holly. *Not God's Type: A Rational Academic Finds a Radical Faith*. Chicago: Moody, 2010.

Tickle, Phyllis. *The Divine Hours (Volume Two): Prayers for Autumn and Wintertime: A Manual for Prayer*. New York: Image, 2006.

Gregory of Nyssa. *The Life of Moses*. Mahwah, N.J.: Paulist Press, 1978.

Maximus the Confessor. *Maximus the Confessor: Selected Writings*. Mahwah, N.J.: Paulist Press, 1985.

Davie, Donald, ed. *The New Oxford Book of Christian Verse*. Oxford: Oxford University Press, 2003.

Six — CONVERSION

Evans, Rachel Held. *Evolving in Monkey Town: How a Girl Who Knew All the Answers Learned to Ask the Questions.* Grand Rapids, Mich.: Zondervan, 2010.

McLaren, Brian D. *A New Kind of Christianity: Ten Questions That Are Transforming the Faith.* San Francisco: HarperOne, 2010.

Weil, Simone. *Need for Roots.* New York: Routledge, 2001.

Didion, Joan. *The Year of Magical Thinking.* New York: Vintage, 2007.

Bynum, Caroline Walker. *Jesus as Mother: Studies in the Spirituality of the High Middle Ages.* Chicago: University of Chicago Press, 1984.

Seven — WALLS

Lewis, C. S. *The Screwtape Letters.* New York: HarperCollins, 2001.

Norris, Richard A., Jr. *The Christological Controversy.* Louisville: Minneapolis: Fortress, 1980.

Endo, Shusaku. *Silence.* Marlboro, N.J.: Taplinger, 1980.

Pseudo-Dionysius. *Pseudo-Dionysius: The Complete Works.* Paul Rorem, trans. Mahwah, N.J.: Paulist Press, 1988.

O'Connor, Flannery. *The Complete Stories.* New York: Farrar, Straus and Giroux, 1971.

Eight — REPENTANCE

L'Engle, Madeleine. *Walking on Water: Meditations on Faith and Art.* New York: North Point Press, 1995.

Marquez, Gabriel Garcia. *One Hundred Years of Solitude.* New York: Harper Perennial, 2006.

Greene, Graham. *The Power and the Glory.* New York: Penguin Classics, 2003.

Balthasar, Hans Urs von. *Mysterium Paschale: The Mystery of Easter.* San Francisco: Ignatius, 2000.

Martel, Yann. *Beatrice and Virgil.* New York: Spiegel & Grau, 2010.

Nine — GRACE

Winner, Lauren. *Girl Meets God: On the Path to a Spiritual Life.* Chapel Hill, N.C.: Algonquin, 2004.

L'Engle, Madeleine. *Penguins and Golden Calves: Icons and Idols in Antarctica and Other Unexpected Places*. Wheaton, Ill.: Shaw, 1996.

Barth, Karl. *Church Dogmatics, III.1, The Doctrine of Creation*. Peabody, Mass.: Hendrickson, 1975.

Tresmontant, Claude. *The Hebrew Christ: Language in the Age of the Gospels*. Chicago: Franciscan Herald, 1989.

MacBeth, Sybil. *Praying in Color*. Brewster, Mass.: Paraclete, 2007.

Ten — TABLES

Percy, Walker. *Love in the Ruins*. New York: Picador, 1999.

Athanasius. *On the Incarnation*. Yonkers, N.Y.: St. Vladimir's Seminary, 1996.

Rubenstein, Jeffrey L., and Shaye J. D. Cohen, eds. *Rabbinic Stories (Classics of Western Spirituality)*. Mahwah, N.J.: Paulist Press, 2002.

Berry, Wendell. *A Timbered Choir: The Sabbath Poems 1979–1997*. Washington, D.C.: Counterpoint, 1999.

Voskamp, Ann. *One Thousand Gifts: A Dare to Live Fully Right Where You Are*. Grand Rapids, Mich.: Zondervan, 2011.

ACKNOWLEDGMENTS

I give thanks to and for:

Hilary, bone of my bone and flesh of my flesh, the peace of my heart and the fullness of my love.

My parents, who taught me righteousness is patient and quiet work; who teach me still.

Sam, my brother, who has seen my worst and my best and still stuck around; who knows all my tricks and calls me out every time I try to use them; who taught me what it means to hope.

Grant, Jerry, and Antonia, the best of friends and the loudest of hearts. Everyone needs one of them. I'm convinced.

My agent, John Topliff, and my editor, John Sloan, and the wonderful team at Zondervan and HarperCollins, who believed in this little book back when it was a sample chapter and a poorly structured book proposal. You all changed my life. (I'm still waiting for you to tell me it was a mistake.)

My eternal love and thanks to Baylor University, particularly Dr. Ralph Wood, Dr. David Lyle Jeffrey, Dr. Sarah-Jane Murray, Tommye Lou Davis, Dr. Gabrielle Sutherland, Dr. Robert Miner, Eileen Bentsen, Zack, Crina, Maggie, Wylie, Joy, Maddee, Caroline, Rachel, Brittany, countless others, and the Great Texts Department as a whole. No one could have dreamed of a better department or a better program. And the Honors Residential College, the best place to live and grow in university years, hands down.

An impossible amount of thanks to my not-so-older-older-sisters — or so I call them — Nish and Sarah, my first editor and my first spiritual director, who have listened to me rant, pushed me to be better, and taught me the way of grace.

I will always treasure Sunday nights at my apartment at the end of the world the year I lived in Scotland, and the remarkable hearts of Paul, Spencer, Denny, Jon, and Emma, who taught me much about careful words, the want of beautiful things, and the iridescent spark of hopefulness.

I don't know what I would have done this past year without Seth, Troy, Chad, and Mike. You're my people. Simple as that.

I am eternally grateful to my online communities, particularly the lavish and loud grace of A Deeper Story and the circles where unicorns are set ablaze with glitter. They have challenged me, called me out, loved me, and taught me to laugh away the dark.

I am thankful for all who, years ago, supported a Kickstarter that allowed me to move to Scotland and draft the first pages that would eventually become this book. It was a long, winding, impossible road, but their gracious support laid the groundwork of a land that I could not even imagine I would get to explore.

To St. Paul's Episcopal Church in Waco, Texas, and Hope-Pointe Anglican Church in The Woodlands, Texas, and all other churches I sojourned on this journey, my love and thanksgiving for the good work you do.

I have the most extraordinary blog readers. Without them, there would be no book. I should say more, praise more, but I think it's best summed up by saying without them I would not have the opportunity to share these words. They best me daily.

Last, I would like to thank my Lord Jesus Christ, the First and the Last, in whom all things hold together, and who reigns forever until he is all in all, in the unity of the Father and the Holy Ghost, forever and ever, world without end, amen.

READING GUIDE AND QUESTIONS

1. Preston explores and describes different forms of *hearing* God—in Scripture, written prayers, almost audibly, as a gut feeling. How do you hear God? Or, do you think people can hear God?

2. Have you ever felt called upon to do a big, dramatic project of God—like The Well—only to feel like it fell apart? How did you reconcile the alleged calling of God with the failing?

3. The Eucharist, Communion, is particularly important to Preston's spiritual journey and is a significant factor in where he ultimately decides to make his denominational home. After reading the book, how do you see Communion in relation to the mission of the Church and Christ's presence within and through it?

4. Early on in the book, Preston struggles to reconcile some of the traditions of evangelical youth culture—short-term missions, testimonials—with the richness that Christian faith has to offer. What do you see as the good and the shortcomings of these practices?

5. Books play a significant role in shaping Preston's perspective on Christianity. What books have been significant to your own faith story?

6. Preston's theology was shaped largely not just by the places he worshiped but by the people he worshiped with. How do

you think theology should be formed? Should it be handed down from an institution or corporately constructed? A blend of both?

7. Sam, Grant, Antonia, and Jerry all play significant roles in Preston's life throughout the course of the book in specific ways, particularly focused on refining and shaping his spirituality. Who has been significant in your life in that way?

8. The word *evangelical* doesn't become a good word to Preston again until late in the book. What words or ideas in Christianity are still sensitive for you?

9. The "walls of Zion" describe for Preston the boundaries of Christian faith and practice, the non-negotiable of belief. What are the walls of Zion for you? Do you have any? Do you believe they are good to have?

10. Father Chuck encourages Preston to settle down denominationally because it is a faithful way of rooting to a people, of taking their bad with their good. What bad in Christianity is difficult for you to sit with. Have you ever thought about it?

NOTES

1. Simone Weil, *Waiting for God* (New York: HarperCollins, 2009), 8.
2. Psalm 78:19 NASB.
3. Psalm 46:10 NIV.
4. Exodus 19:17a NASB.
5. Exodus 20:1–2 NASB.
6. The text of Lauren's sermon can be found on the Duke Divinity School chapel website: chapel.duke.edu/sites/default/files/Winner—Exodus20.pdf.
7. Exodus Rabbah 29:9, quoted in Lawrence Kushner, *I'm God, You're Not: Observations on Organized Religion* (Woodstock, Vt.: Jewish Lights, 2010), 193.
8. Exodus 20:20 NASB.
9. Habakkuk 2:20 NASB.
10. Habakkuk 1:2 NASB.
11. Hebrews 3:15 NIV.
12. Ross King, "Meet with Me."
13. Chris Tomlin, "In the Secret."
14. Psalm 22:3 KJV.
15. Psalm 43:5 KJV.
16. Gerard Manley Hopkins, "God's Grandeur," *The Poems of Gerard Manley Hopkins* (London: Oxford University Press, 1967), 66.
17. Habakkuk 1:5 ESV.
18. From the original prologue of the Harley Mss 978 including Marie de France's Lais; translation my own.
19. I first learned this turn of phrase from Joy Bennet, who penned the remarkable, "I Am Not Your Holy Spirit" for *A Deeper Story* in November 2011, deeperstory .com/i-am-not-your-holy-spirit/
20. "The Genoa Tip," *The Newsroom*, Season 2, Episode 2 (HBO. July 21, 2013).
21. A play on the title of Marshall Berman's fascinating *All That Is Solid Melts into Air: The Experience of Modernity* (London: Penguin, 1988).
22. See the compilation of Dr. John Kruse, *Lent and Easter Wisdom from St. Francis and St. Clare of Assisi* (Rome: Liguori, 2008).
23. Elizabeth Barrett Browning, *Aurora Leigh*, 86.61–62.

24. Wisdom of Solomon 16:20–21 NRSV.

25. Sirach 10:12 NRSV.

26. Charles Taylor, *A Secular Age* (Cambridge, Mass.: The Belknap Press of Harvard University Press, 2007), 25.

27. John Milton, *Paradise Lost* VII.96–97.

28. *Oxford Dictionary of Quotations*, 7th ed. (London: Oxford University Press, 2009), 684. For more on Teresa of Ávila, see *Teresa of Ávila: Interior Castle (Classics of Western Spirituality)* (Mahwah, N.J.: Paulist Press, 1979).

29. 1 Peter 3:20–21 NRSV.

30. Madeleine L'Engle, *Walking on Water* (New York: North Point Press, 1995), 50.

31. Gjertrud Schnackenberg, "Sonata," *Supernatural Love: Poems 1976–1992* (New York: Farrar, Straus & Giroux, 2000), 102.

32. Thomas Aquinas, adapting the cosmological argument of Aristotle.

33. Francis of Assisi and Clare of Assisi, *Francis and Clare: The Complete Works (Classics of Western Spirituality)*, trans. Regis J. Armstrong and Ignatius C. Brady (Mahwah, N.J.: Paulist Press, 1986), 63. For a good compilation of the writings of Francis and Clare, see also John Kruse, *Lent and Easter Wisdom From St. Francis and St. Clare of Assisi (Lent & Easter Wisdom)* (Liguori, Mo.: Liguroi, 2008).

34. Simone Weil, *Waiting for God* (New York: HarperCollins, 2009), 8.

35. John 6:51 NRSV.

36. Psalm 48:12–14 NRSV.

37. See Nahum N. Glatzer, *Language of Faith: A Selection from the Most Expressive Jewish Prayers* (New York: Schocken Books Inc., 1947), 94.

38. See John Kruse's compilation, *Lent and Easter Wisdom From St. Francis and St. Clare of Assisi (Lent & Easter Wisdom)* (Liguori, Mo.: Liguroi, 2008).

39. Michael O'Brien, *Father Elijah: An Apocalypse* (San Francisco: Ignatius Press, 1997), 192.